American Harvest

Regional Recipes
for the
Vegetarian Kitchen

Also by Nava Atlas

Vegetariana
A Rich Harvest of Wit, Lore and Recipes

Vegetarian Celebrations
Menus for Holidays and Other Festive Occasions

Soups for All Seasons
Bountiful Vegetarian Soups

American Harvest

Regional Recipes
for the
Vegetarian Kitchen

Written and Illustrated by
NAVA ATLAS

Amberwood Press
New Paltz, NY

American Harvest

Regional Recipes for the Vegetarian Kitchen

Copyright © 1987 by Nava Atlas

Second Edition copyright © 1991

Cover and text design by Nava Atlas

Library of Congress Catalog Card Number: 86-91069

ISBN: 0-9630243-0-2

Printed in the United States of America

10 9 8 7 6 5 4 3

For my mother

Doing a book that is a collection of lore and recipes handed down from the past and updated for the future is a joy, since the information comes from diverse and fascinating sources. Many people contributed not only their knowledge but also fond memories of the foods they grew up with, some of which have remained a part of their lives as an ongoing tradition.

Among the many people who offered information, I'd like to mention the following for contributing recipes or for taking time out from their busy schedules to talk to me about the foods of their region: Suzanne Carney; the staff of the Coffee Pot restaurant in New Orleans; Mildred "Dip," of Dip's Country Kitchen in Chapel Hill (I'm sorry I couldn't catch her last name); Amina DaDa, of I & I Creole Vegetarian Restaurant in New Orleans; Sharon Dowell, food editor of the *Oklahoma City Daily Oklahoman*; Barbara Freer, of Mainstreet Bakery in Taos; Grand America restaurant in New York City; Alvaro Jurado; F. Leo Kendall, of the Apple Tree restaurant in Taos; Barbara McPhail; Henry Nelson; Russ Parsons, food editor of the *Albuquerque Tribune*; and Anne Phillips, food editor of the *Atlanta Constitution*. A very special mention must go to Jane Lovato, who shared much information on the foods of the Southwest.

No matter how many people one might talk to, it would be impossible to get a sense of the past without digging into the books of those times. I'd like to acknowledge the New York Public Library, whose incredible collection of original old American cookbooks contributed much to this one. I'd also like to mention the following special libraries and institutions, whose collections and displays were not only highly informative but a pleasure to visit: the Atlanta Historical Society; Colonial Williamsburg (Virginia); the Historic New Orleans Collection, with special thanks to Jessica Travis; and the Walter C. Jackson Library of the University of North Carolina at Greensboro.

Personal thanks go to my editor, Ginny Faber. I'm grateful to Diana Price, whose friendship and support are well beyond an agent's call of duty, and to Patrick Bunyan for his research contributions. Finally, my husband, Chaim Tabak, is to be thanked profusely for accompanying me on 6,500 miles of travels (actually, he did most of the driving), for being a most discerning taster, and for getting me a word processor for my birthday.

CONTENTS

American Harvest

Regional Recipes
for the
Vegetarian Kitchen

INTRODUCTION

Oh! how my heart sighs for my own native land,
　Where potatoes, and squashes, and cucumbers grow;
Where cheer and good welcome are always at hand,
　And custards, and pumpkin pies smoke in a row;
Where pudding the visage of hunger serenes,
　And, what is far better, the pot of baked beans.

—*The New England Farmer*, 1829

Pick up any vegetarian cookbook and you will most likely find an enticing array of ethnic recipes—Italian, Chinese, and Indian are just a few of the cuisines whose influence has enlivened the vegetarian repertoire and made the meatless alternative more attractive to the general public than was the "soybeans and oats" school of the sixties. The appeal of foreign dishes has helped make us a nation of enlightened eaters, vegetarian or not. The emphasis on interesting combinations of fresh vegetables, exotic seasonings, and delectable grain and legume dishes proved that a lighter diet, whether a full-time or a part-time one, is far from boring.

Just as all of these exotic new cuisines seemed to settle into a comfortable niche in this nation's eating habits, there seemed to be a sudden explosion of interest in regional and traditional American cookery. Seemingly overnight, a number of fascinating books and a proliferation of articles appeared on the subject, almost as a reminder to preserve and continue the tradition of down-home classics that developed, so to speak, in our own backyards. I enjoyed reading these writings—somehow, they made me feel warm and nostalgic and evoked images of charming small towns and Thanksgiving at grandmother's. This was a strange effect to be worked on me, a child of immigrants, myself not even American born!

My interest led me to wonder whether a complete selection of American recipes, from soup to nuts, could be tailored to the vegetarian kitchen. And of course, the answer is a resounding yes.

The criterion for choosing the recipes in this book was that they fit in with today's emphasis on healthy, lighter eating, with lots of fresh vegetables, fruits, grains, and legumes. Though these items may not come immediately to mind when one thinks "American food," they once played a *major* role in the traditional diet. Before the turn of the century, meat was often just one component of a meal or a dish, rather than its focal point. It was the age of affluence that altered our eating habits in this century.

Wholesome recipes abound among the regional styles represented here, which include those from New England, the South, the Pennsylvania Dutch, the Southwest, the Creole of New Orleans, and the vast "heartland" of America. Though the culinary approaches differ widely, there is a strong thread running through the recipes, represented by the use of the fresh ingredients that constitute our native harvest. Among these are included beans and peas of every color, corn utilized in a wide range of forms (from fresh off the cob to snowy grits); an abundance of squashes, rice, sweet and white potatoes; an assortment of fruits that fill every manner of traditional dessert; and a bounty of vegetables for every season. From these ingredients are assembled a profusion of dishes, ranging from simple and earthy to exotic and elegant, that will be welcomed by vegetarians and healthy-food lovers alike: great whole-grain breads and muffins; warming soups, both plain and fancy; flavorful, protein-rich grain and bean entrees; delectable egg and dairy specialties; satisfying low-sugar sweets; and much more.

Now you can add to your repertoire of Italian pastas, Chinese stir fries, and Indian curries an array of tempting homegrown classics such as southwestern enchiladas, thick Creole soups, southern griddlecakes, and New England pies. And, as an added relish, you can sample the surprising and fascinating lore and literature that have accompanied the development of American cooking since its inception.

THE COLONIAL EDEN

The story of colonial agriculture and cookery is familiar to those of us who were American schoolchildren. It begins with the well-known fact that the early European settlers, arriving in a vast, untamed land, would have starved if not for the guidance they received from the Indians. From them the colonists learned how to hunt the land, sky, and seas for game, fowl, and fish and to discern which wild plants yielded edible nuts, berries, and greens.

The greatest gift that the native Americans passed along to the settlers was the ability to cultivate and utilize corn. No other single food item had so great an impact on the development of American cookery. Corn quickly became a staple crop for the colonists, as it required little skill in cultivation. It grew well even in poor soil and produced a food that was as versatile as it was nutritious. As an added bonus to corn cultivation, beans and squash could be grown among the rows of corn, their vines and stalks intertwining. Corn, beans, and squash have long been known as "the three sisters" in many branches of Indian mythology; these life-sustaining crops are represented by three daughters of the Earth Mother who protect the harvest.

The early years of colonization could not have been a paradise for the newcomers, fraught as they were with the hardships of adjustment to a drastically different way of life. But, in time, the knowledge learned from the Indians, combined with the familiarity of the settlers with certain native crops that had been carried back to Europe by earlier travelers (these include several varieties of beans, sweet peppers, pumpkins and other squashes, and white and sweet potatoes) ensured that the new land would be generous. Eventually the settlers added to these crops plants from seeds they had brought from Europe, including several types of cabbage, lettuce, peas, and herbs.

By the early 1700s, two chroniclers of colonial Virginia set down descriptions of the agriculture of that area in exquisite detail, painting a picture of a veritable Eden of produce. In fact, William

Byrd's *Natural History of Virginia* (1737), is subtitled, "or the Newly Discovered Eden." Byrd's report of what he saw being grown at that time, makes today's supermarket offerings pale in comparison. Here is his description of what he refers to merely as "pot herbs," presumably a list of what was grown in some kitchen gardens:

> Turnips, carrots, beets, four species of cabbage, such as smooth savoy cabbage, curled red, curled green, as also beautiful cauliflower, chives, artichokes, radish, horseradish, many species of potatoes . . . parsnips . . . white and red garlic . . . smooth, curled and red lettuce, round and prickly spinach, two kinds of fennel . . . cultivated and wild rhubarb, sorrel, two kinds of cress, mustard, two species of parsley, very large and long asparagus of splendid flavor, white as well as red. There are many species of melons, Guinea, golden, orange, green, and several other sorts. There are three varieties of cucumbers, which are very sweet and good-tasting; four species of pumpkins . . . squashes are also very good, raw or cooked. All these are Indian vegetables or pot herbs; therefore [they are] not at all or imperfectly known. In addition, there are still many other garden stuffs, which would take too long to mention here.

Byrd stresses the importance of corn as a staple crop for the multitudes, saying,:

> This corn is very good in this land and is eaten by everyone, rich or poor. People consider it very healthful. . . . Indeed most of the inhabitants plant almost nothing but corn for their household needs, with which they are pleased and remain healthy besides. Their intention in this is that it is much less trouble to plant and offers more advantages than grain, since corn yields the planter in good soil seven to eight hundredfold or still more.

Other grain crops mentioned are wheat, rye, barley, and oats, but none are emphasized or described as much as corn.

Robert Beverly's tract on the same subject, *The History and Present State of Virginia* (1705), predates Byrd's by some years but offers a no-less-detailed description of the agricultural bounty of Virginia. The number of different types of fruit trees alone, with all their species and subspecies, is astonishing. He is able to identify, for example, twenty-five different types of pears! Like Byrd, Beverly tells of the importance of corn, relating it to the lives of the Indians:

> This Indian Corn was the Staff of Food, upon which the Indians did ever depend; for when sickness, bad weather, war or any other ill Accident kept them from Hunting, Fishing and Fowling; this, with the Addition of some Peas, Beans and such other fruits of the Earth, as were then in season, was the Families Dependence, and the Support of their Women and Children.

Later in the same century, in this surrounding of variety and abundance, the self-described Virginia "epicurean," Thomas Jefferson, was nurtured. Despite the fact that his career was devoted to law and politics, Jefferson's early ambition was to be a gentleman planter. His love of fine food seemed almost innate, and his creativity as a gardener is well documented in his *Garden Books* (1766–1824). In his gardens grew cucumbers, cabbage, spinach, sprouts, squashes, potatoes, artichokes, lettuce, cauliflower, eggplant, endive, onions, turnips, beets, and much more. Even the ordinary vegetables were classified as to their exact variety—"Carrots from Pisa, Salmon radishes, Lattuga lettuce, Windsor beans, cluster peas . . . "

Jefferson also grew a wide variety of legumes, including the green peas that he so loved, as well as lentils, black-eyed peas, and several varieties of beans. His enthusiasm extended also to his lovely orchards, which bore a multitude of fruits and nuts. The tables set by Jefferson were in such style and taste that it has been said that their quality, both in and out of the White House, has rarely been matched. His overseer, Bacon, commented that "He was never a great eater, but what he did eat he wanted to be very choice."

The first truly regional American cookbook to reflect the culinary diversity of its area appeared near the end of the Jeffersonian era. It was *The Virginia Housewife* by Mary Randolph, first published in 1824. Mrs. Randolph, a member of a prominent Virginia family, conveys a sense of the lavish diversity of local foods and a great deal of sensitivity to the quality of ingredients. Although largely based on cooking techniques brought over from England, Mrs. Randolph's book includes a profusion of New World foods. Meat and fish abound in her pages, to be sure, but the sheer variety of fruits, vegetables, and grains used in her recipes dispels any notion of a universally lackluster early American table. Hearty breads, elegant desserts bursting with luscious berries and other fruits, pickles, relishes, beautifully seasoned soups, and numerous other enticing selections make it a cookbook that is still useful.

Mrs. Randolph's cookbook must have inspired some of the superb ones that followed hers later in the nineteenth century, such as Eliza Leslie's *Directions for Cookery*, which went through several editions in mid-century, and Maria Parloa's *Miss Parloa's Kitchen Companion* (1887). In poring over those as well as scores of other culinary volumes of that period, I discovered a fascinating world of sensible yet creative cooks who used our native harvest to its full advantage. Their words and ideas, forgotten for so long, are, happily, being rediscovered and are proving to be deliciously timeless.

A VEGETARIAN'S-EYE VIEW OF AMERICAN REGIONAL CUISINES

In this collection, recipes from a wide range of sources, utilizing diverse cooking techniques and having disparate histories, are meshed together. However, you will find that what they have in common prevails over their differences, since similar ingredients often find their way from one cuisine to another. Of course, there are variations in seasoning—from bland to fiery—preferences in cooking styles, and occasional food items that are unique to one region. No differences, though, however subtle or obvious, will overshadow the freshness and basic unpretentiousness of the recipes as a whole. So, before all these recipes wind up under the umbrella of "regional American vegetarian," here is a brief description of the regional cuisines represented in this book, with a view to what each has to offer to the vegetarian palate.

NEW ENGLAND

Old New England—the phrase calls to mind small towns nestled among mountains, steepled white churches, and vibrantly colored autumn leaves. New England food just as quickly brings to mind a set of firmly planted ideas, calling forth images of the boiled dinner, with its corned beef and root vegetables, as well as codfish balls and seafood chowders. Digging beyond the obvious, though, this simple cuisine of Puritan roots has some worthy treasures to contribute to the vegetarian kitchen.

Colonial New England was not as bountiful a land as the early Virginia described in previous pages. The reason was simple: the climate was harsher, and thus the soil was suited best to hardier crops. Added to this, fireplace cooking with the "spider-legged" skillets and black iron pots, along with the Puritan penchant for simplicity, dictated that the most practical dishes were plain and long-cooking.

What I found most useful in the range of New England recipes was the number of ideas for using winter vegetables. The much-maligned parsnip is turned into an elegant and warming chowder. Similarly, such other common vegetables as potatoes, cabbage, and beets are turned into comforting classics that take the doldrums out of cold-weather cooking. Another nice contribution was a group of interesting and fortifying pancakes, sweetened with maple syrup, a New England perennial. The crowning touch of the region's staples is none other than its great American pies and fruit desserts. Brimming with apples, blueberries, cranberries, strawberries, pumpkin, squash, and bananas, these desserts make it possible to enjoy a sweet treat without feeling sinful!

PENNSYLVANIA DUTCH

The Pennsylvania Dutch are descendants of German immigrants who arrived in this country in the seventeenth century. Thus the term *Dutch* is a misnomer and actually a corruption of *Deutsch,* meaning "German." Their cookery developed as an adaptation of the German style as applied to the agricultural and climatic conditions of the areas they settled, predominantly Pennsylvania, with pockets in Ohio, Indiana, and Iowa. The Dutch were (and still are in large part) a self-sustaining farm people whose Amish and Mennonite branches are the best known. Their penchant for plain living and the isolation of farm life during long winters resulted in a style of cooking that is simple, filling, and strength-giving.

It is a fascinating and underexplored cuisine, and the hardy crops basic to New England are equally prominent here. Scrapple and pepper pot might spring to mind immediately as characteristic Dutch dishes, but corn, potatoes, cabbage, apples, parsnips, and egg noodles form the basis of many hearty dishes a vegetarian can enjoy. It's hard to go wrong with such classics as Corn Noodles, Dutch Succotash, Red Wine Cabbage, and Potato-Bread Stuffing, among others with similarly "homey" evocations.

The true artistry of Dutch cooking, the ability to stretch homegrown food from season to season by drying, canning, and pickling foods (hence the famous relishes known as the seven sweets and seven sours), is an aspect you might like to explore if this particular cuisine catches your fancy.

THE SOUTH

In no other regional style is there the vast amount of specific foods used as there is in southern cookery. As described in the previous pages, colonial Virginia was a haven of produce, and this was true of many other parts of the South, with its climate so favorable to growing both wild and cultivated foods. This variety of foods native to the southern soil by way of the Indians was combined with the foods brought over as part of the slave trade from Africa (for instance, okra, peanuts, and black-eyed peas). Prepare these foods in the earthy style of southern blacks or in the carried-over European manner of the wealthy planter families, and sometimes a little of both, and you have the basic components of southern cooking.

The repertoire of the South is very wide-ranging. The foods that are now the basis of "soul food" formed the core of the diet of southern blacks from the days of slavery: greens, black-eyed peas, sweet potatoes, cornbread, grits, and various forms of salt meat. These foods and their preparation have survived to become an integral part of any "typical" southern menu, crossing any boundary of class or race. Conversely, the penchant of the wealthier planters for "big eating," where quantity is almost as important as quality, is reflected in the menus of even the humblest of diners in the South today.

During my southern travels, I noticed on any menu considered traditional, no matter how simple the establishment, a long list of daily vegetables, from which one could choose four or five at a set price. At one such place in South Carolina, the list read like this: lima beans, turnip greens with turnips, candied yams, pickled beets, cole slaw, crowder peas, hush puppies (fried cornmeal balls), and banana pudding. Other lists would include black-eyed peas, collard greens, string beans, corn, potato salad, cauliflower, and broccoli. Dessert standards were most always sweet potato pie and pecan pie. As vegetarians, we would have to avoid the beans (including string beans), peas, and greens because they are invariably "seasoned," as it is called, with salt pork or bacon. This illustrates, however, the love of hearty food, and lots of it!

I've already mentioned quite a number of foods typical to southern cooking, and these played an important role in the recipes that I chose for this collection. Many of my adaptations will lighten the dishes, keeping them low in fat and high in flavor. Of great interest to me were dishes incorporating sweet potatoes, a highly nutritious but underutilized crop, as well as those including the great variety of beans and peas, which have been a pillar of the cookery of this region. Corn plays as crucial a role in southern cooking as it does in most any other region's and yields several wonderful classic inventions. Biscuits, corn breads and other hearty breads, griddle cakes, cole slaws, and fruity desserts were also among the generous bounty of great classics from this region that fit in beautifully with this collection.

CREOLE COOKERY

William Makepeace Thackeray, the British author, found New Orleans to be "of all the cities in the world, where you can eat the most and suffer the least." New Orleans is the hub of Creole culture, and it is there that its distinctive cookery was born.

Creoles are the descendants of the Spanish and French settlers of Louisiana in its Colonial period. They're also the descendants of the West Indian or African blacks who settled the area or were taken as slaves. Futher, with the centuries of intermixing of these groups, it might suffice to say that a Creole is the descendant of a true native of Louisiana, no matter what color or extraction. This excludes the Cajuns, whose ancestors, the Acadians of Nova Scotia, settled and farmed Louisiana's lush Bayou country.

The Creole and Cajun cooking styles have much in common, with many overlapping ingredients. Perhaps the essential difference might be summed up in saying that whereas the Creole aspires to elegance, Cajun cookery is its more rustic, earthy counterpart. It was much more difficult to extract from the latter typical dishes that could be adapted for vegetarians; almost always pungent and fiery, the Cajun repertoire makes constant use of all the sea life so abundant in the area. That, along with the use of peppery homemade sausage, put too distinct a stamp on their dishes to encourage me to attempt to adapt many of them.

Creole cooking incorporates elements of French haute cuisine, the Spanish and African love of high seasoning, the West Indian way with exotic herbs, and the lavish supply of ingredients basic to the American South. Central to this style is the talent for seasoning, ranging from delicate to fiery, but always making a statement. The 1941 Works Progress Administration guide to Louisiana comments that "well stocked as the larder may be, it is the seasoning that makes Creole food distinctive. Onions, garlic, bay leaf, celery, red, green, black and cayenne pepper, parsley, thyme, shallots, basil, cloves, nutmeg and allspice are used in different combinations."

New Orleans has long been known as an eater's city, but it is not a vegetarian's paradise. My husband and I loaded up on the fabulous breakfasts because we were rather limited for our other meals—Creole restaurant cooking today is quite dominated by the abundant and diverse seafood of the area. Even the famous stuffed vegetables are filled with shrimp or crab. Happily, but a bit too late in our visit, we discovered the I & I Creole Vegetarian Restaurant on Saint Peter Street, where we enjoyed owner Amina DaDa's interpretations of classics of the area and her stories of her efforts to introduce these adapted standards to a resistant public! More of her comments and recipe ideas will be seen later.

Creole home cooking, much of it documented in charming turn-of-the-century cookbooks, provided the basis, then, for the recipes that I've adapted. Great soups and vegetable dishes were high on my list of favorites, being perfect beneficiaries of the Creole genius for seasoning. Dishes incorporating another Louisiana staple, rice, were also welcome, especially when combined with beans, as in the famous Red Beans and Rice. Further, the Creole is the only American cuisine that has adopted the eggplant and provides several very special and unusual recipes for it. After a stroll in the French Quarter, there was no more pleasant way for us to end the day than with a nice piece of aromatic Bread Pudding laced with a sauce of rum or whiskey. This seductive treat is included in the desserts chapter as a reminder of New Orleans' slightly decadent side.

THE SOUTHWEST

The Southwest, with its warm, languid days and cool desert nights, has produced a cuisine that is down-to-earth, yet at the same time, terribly exotic. Based on centuries-old food customs of the Pueblo Indians, the arrival of the Spanish missionaries brought with it their preference for highly seasoned food and the means with which to make it so, along with a few other staples to add to the repertoire. Added to this is additional produce and culinary influence from Mexico, and the result is a rich, distinct range of recipes with a great deal of simplicity, style, and integrity.

Tex-Mex is not a term I will use very much; it's vague and often used as a catchall. Suffice it to say that the questions as to the differences between the cooking styles of Texas, New Mexico, Arizona, and California, as well as what developed north or south of the border are hotly debated ones. The recipes in this collection represent those that are common to the area in general.

The Southwest is an adventurous vegetarian's haven in a sea of coast-to-coast homogeneity. There's lots to choose from, and many restaurants are lightening up the classics, such as preparing refried pinto beans with vegetable oil instead of lard. These well-loved, *ubiquitous frijoles*, along with tortilla specialties such as enchiladas or burritos and rice, are often the basis of a filling, high-protein meal. Add to these staples green chiles (lots of them!) tomatoes, onions, garlic, bell pepper, cheese, squashes, avocado, potatoes, garbanzos, and black beans, and you've got the basis for any number of exciting variations.

Tortilla specialties notwithstanding, the Southwest has also made quite a few lively contributions to this collection in the form of unusual egg dishes, well-seasoned soups, and robust salads, among others. If my preference for this region's cookery peeks through, forgive me—it's irresistible, and once you're hooked, you'll know what I mean.

NOTES ON INGREDIENTS

Here is a list of ingredients used commonly or occasionally in the recipes that warrant some discussion. Refer to this list for additional information that may come in handy.

FLOURS, MEALS, AND GRAINS

Buckwheat flour

This is used to make buckwheat cakes and has a very assertive flavor. Buy it in one- or two-pound bags at health food stores.

Cornmeal

Buy stone-ground or water-ground meal at health food stores. The commercial variety has been bolted of its valuable germ. White or yellow cornmeal may be used interchangeably in the recipes.

Masa harina

Used for making corn tortillas, this is limed cornmeal that is especially prepared for this purpose. If you'd like to try making tortillas at home, masa is marketed by Quaker Oats in five-pound bags. Look for it in supermarkets or in Mexican specialty groceries.

Rice

I always recommend brown rice, whose nutritious hull has been kept on, giving it a nutty flavor and preventing it from becoming starchy and sticky when cooking. Rice swells to about two and a half times its original bulk when cooked. Cover it in water in a two and a half-to-one ratio, then simmer over low heat, covered, until the water has been absorbed, about 35 to 40 minutes.

Whole wheat flour

Used in whole or part in bread and dessert recipes, buy it in bulk at health or natural food stores, or in two- or five-pound bags in supermarkets.

Unbleached white flour

This is used to cut the heaviness of whole wheat flour in desserts and in some breads and also as a thickener for sauces.

Beans and Peas

Black beans
Black-eyed peas
Cowpeas
Garbanzo beans (chick-peas)

Navy or small white beans
Pinto beans
Red or kidney beans

All of the above are used in the recipes. First, I'd like to say a few kind words on behalf of the poor, maligned beans, which seem to have a false reputation for being "fattening," much the way pasta has had until recently. That they are filling and bulky should not be confused with their being heavy, which they aren't. A serving of beans or peas is very low in calories, and the fat content is almost nil!

The cooking method I like best is as follows: Sort and rinse the beans or peas and soak them overnight in plenty of water. When you're ready to cook them, drain and rinse them again and add water in at least one and one-half times their bulk. Cook over low heat, covered. Pinto, red, and kidney beans require about 1½ to 2 hours, garbanzos at least 2 hours. Black beans, navy beans, black-eyed peas, and cowpeas generally require 1 to 1½ hours. This will all vary according to how long you've soaked the beans, the temperature at which they are cooked, and even the altitude at which you live! Test the beans occasionally toward the end of the cooking times recommended—they should be soft and mealy when pressed between thumb and forefinger. You don't want them to be mushy, but neither should they be underdone—that makes them hard to digest.

Some other tips: Add salt only toward the end of the cooking. Also, for added flavor and softer texture, add a small onion cut in half and 1 or 2 tablespoons of safflower oil to the water when you begin to cook the beans. These beans and peas generally yield from 2¼ to 2½ times their original bulk when cooked, hence, 1 cup of dried will equal 2¼ to 2½ cups when cooked. These all freeze well, so cook extra, and save the flavorful cooking water to use as soup stock.

Canned beans

All of the above beans and peas come in canned form. In a pinch, or when small amounts are needed, using canned beans is fine as long as you choose a brand without additives. The drawback to canned beans is that they're high in sodium.

Green peas

Fresh green peas are best. Besides, it's fun to nibble on raw peas while shelling them. The season for fresh peas is late spring to early summer.

Lima beans

It's nearly impossible to find fresh lima beans, so the frozen variety, called green baby lima beans, will do. They are often on the underdone side, which is good, so that further stewing and simmering does not kill them. Many folks, myself included, don't go for the dried white limas, which tend to be grainy and flavorless.

Corn and Corn Products

Fresh corn

Get into the habit of scraping corn kernels right off the cob instead of reaching for frozen corn. Usually you will cook the corn first. Here in New York I've noticed that the corn season has been extended due to imported corn from Florida, and for the most part, this corn is very good. The sweet white corn of late summer is most delicious in recipes where corn is highlighted.

Frozen corn

Use frozen corn only in the winter, and then only in dishes where it is not the main ingredient. Most corn recipes are just not worth making with anything but the fresh, and I'll alert you as the occasions present themselves.

Grits (or hominy grits)

Quaker Oats grits and quick grits are the most readily available. Having eaten a lot of grits in the South, I find that Quaker Oats' product is consistently good.

Tortillas

Corn tortillas are easy to find in your supermarket's frozen-food section, and they're usually acceptable if not spectacular. The adventurous might enjoy making tortillas at home with masa harina (page 9), a tortilla press, and the recipe on page 144.

MISCELLANEOUS INGREDIENTS

Bread crumbs

Rather than throwing out your slightly-dried-out ends of bread, put them to good use by making crumbs. Simply tear leftover bits of whole-grain bread into small pieces and process them in a food processor or blender until finely ground. For crunchier crumbs, first dry the bread out in the oven at a low temperature.

Butter

I agonized over the butter-versus-margarine issue due to the saturated fat and cholesterol content of the former. However, supermarket margarines almost always contain a long list of additives. My compromise is to keep the butter content as low as possible in recipes where it's used. A good alternative is to use soy margarine from health or natural food stores.

Cheeses

The recipes in this book call for either Cheddar or Monterey Jack cheese. That's it! I like to use sharp Cheddar; its flavor goes a long way.

Green chiles

Chiles are the flavoring backbone of southwestern cookery. Experienced cooks with patience and access to fresh chiles will roast and peel them at home, but in most other areas, one is lucky to find chiles at all. Most readily available are those tiny, four-ounce cans that come from the Southwest. The product is good, but for chile lovers, they just don't go very far and are expensive. Green chiles will be labeled mild or hot on the can; you might also try looking for frozen chiles in Mexican specialty stores; they're not as easy to find but are more economical.

Jalapeño peppers

These small, hot chiles seem to be the most readily available of the southwestern varieties. But please, use them only when they're specifically called for, and not interchangeably with green chiles! I like them best when they come marinated in jars. The pickled kind are best used only as garnish.

Nuts

Most often used in these recipes are pecans, with walnuts coming in second. Sunflower seeds are called for on rare occasions. If your kitchen is cool, store the nuts in tightly lidded jars at room temperature; otherwise store them in the refrigerator if they are not used up quickly.

Oils

I recommend safflower oil most often, since it has been praised for being one of the best of the polyunsaturated cooking oils. Its flavor is neutral, very much like your basic vegetable oil. It is available in health food stores and supermarkets. Olive oil is recommended occasionally for recipes that are Spanish-influenced. Virgin or extra-virgin olive oil are best.

Tomatoes

Bright red plum tomatoes are best for cooking (or for using raw, for that matter) since they are juicy and flavorful. Leave them outside the refrigerator in a paper bag for a day or so before cooking with them. I won't be the first or last to advise avoiding those hard hothouse varieties. Canned imported plum tomatoes are good for soups and stews and in general as a substitute for fresh tomatoes for winter cooking.

Vinegar

There seem to be a million different kinds of vinegars nowadays, so I'm almost embarrassed to say that the one I prefer using for these American recipes is plain old apple cider vinegar. I've grown fond of its sweet-sour flavor and think it works nicely as an all-purpose vinegar.

SWEETENERS

Light brown sugar

This is my preferred sweetener for baking. It's not as heavy as honey, and honey has little nutritional edge. The trick is to have sweets in moderation, and when you do, use as little sugar as possible to satisfy your sweet tooth. Honey is used here on some occasions when a little subtle sweetness is needed in cooking or bread baking.

Maple Syrup

Maple syrup is the sweetener for the griddle cakes in chapter 1. Buy pure maple syrup that comes from New England or Canada. It's more expensive, but definitely worth it.

Molasses

Molasses' strong flavor makes people who aren't used to it a little shy of it. If you can acquire a taste for it, so much the better, since it's the only sweetener in common use that has good nutritional value, being high in iron and other minerals. Use unsulfured blackstrap molasses.

HERBS AND SPICES

Here is a list of those seasonings used most commonly in the recipes. Most are ones you would keep on hand in any case.

Allspice
Basil (use fresh as much as possible)
Bay leaves
Black peppers (use whole peppercorns and grind as needed)
Cayenne pepper
Chile powder
Cilantro (this is the fresh leaves of the coriander plant, sometimes called Chinese parsley. Look for it in Mexican or Oriental specialty groceries.)
Cinnamon
Cloves (have both ground and whole on hand)

Cumin
Dill (use it fresh whenever you like)
Dried hot red pepper flakes
Dry mustard
Garlic (use fresh only)
Nutmeg (ground or freshly grated, as you prefer)
Oregano
Paprika
Parsley (use fresh only, preferably the flat-leaf)
Thyme

NOTES ON EQUIPMENT

The recipes in this book require only the most basic of utensils and containers, but I would like to say a few words on behalf of a handful of items that make cooking even more pleasurable.

Double boiler

A double boiler is useful, especially in cooking cornmeal or grits, which burn and stick easily. It's also handy for long-cooking custard sauces which are a part of certain desserts—those, too, are very heat-sensitive.

Oven thermometer

Several friends have complained that their ovens have two temperatures—on and off. This could lead to many a disaster, especially where breadmaking and desserts are concerned. Corn bread, for example, must be baked quickly in a hot oven. A meringue won't set if the oven is not at 425° F. Indian Pudding not baked in a slow 300° F oven will become unpalatably crusty. I, too, have been working with a temperamental oven and have found that the thermometer is a lifesaver. By using it and experimenting with your oven's dial, you'll discover exactly where those elusive temperatures are.

Silverstone cookware

One of the greatest gifts to those of us who enjoy lighter cooking has been Silverstone skillets and other cookware. The durable, nonstick finish makes it easy to cut down on butter and oil, saving lots of fat and calories. Silverstone griddles are wonderful for griddle cakes; and finally (at the risk of sounding like a commercial), Silverstone is a cinch to clean. Silverstone is the name of the nonstick finish; the cookware is marketed under the name of several different manufacturers.

Steamer basket

This handy, inexpensive item is great for preparing perfectly tender-crisp vegetables. Just fill a pot with about 1 inch of water and plunk the steamer in, followed by your vegetables. Steam them, covered, until tender-crisp.

TABLE OF METRIC EQUIVALENTS

The following are metric conversions for those weights and measures used most commonly in this book. The equivalents are close approximations.

Ounces/ Pounds	Grams (g)
4 ounces	115 g
8 ounces	
(½ pound)	225 g
10 ounces	285 g
12 ounces	
(¾ pound)	340 g
16 ounces	
(1 pound)	450 g
24 ounces	
(1½ pounds)	680 g
28 ounces	790 g
32 ounces	
(2 pounds)	900 g

Quarts	Liters
1 quart	1 liter
1½ quarts	1½ liters
2 quarts	2 liters

Inches	Centi- meters (cm)
⅛ inch	½ cm
¼ inch	1 cm
½ inch	1½ cm
1 inch	2½ cm
2 inches	5 cm
3 inches	8 cm
4 inches	10 cm
5 inches	13 cm
6 inches	15 cm
7 inches	18 cm
8 inches	20 cm
9 inches	23 cm
10 inches	25 cm

Fahrenheit (F)	Centigrade (C)
300° F	150° C
325° F	165° C
350° F	180° C
375° F	190° C
400° F	205° C
425° F	220° C

Chapter 1
BISCUITS, MUFFINS, AND GRIDDLECAKES

Who recalls when a girl could hardly wait till she got married so she could make some biscuits?

—Kin Hubbard
Abe Martin on Things in General, 1925

This was a chapter I particularly enjoyed testing, since, like many people, I found myself in a serious "breakfast rut." Busy people these days often gulp down their morning coffee with a little something or other or skip breakfast altogether. In days past, breakfast was a substantial meal, meant to be sustaining for a good day's work. Alice B. Toklas, in her cookbook, recalls that "the first food I remember from my childhood in San Francisco in the [eighteen] eighties is breakfast food . . ." The southern breakfast, too, is especially known for its grand scale.

What a treat it is to wake up to hot whole-grain muffins or biscuits or to a stack of pancakes. No doubt, a bit of planning is required, since few people I know are going to get up early on a weekday morning before their long commute and whip up a batch of muffins! However, muffin batter and biscuit dough take little time to prepare and bake, so why not make them in the evening? It's a relaxing way to unwind, and you can keep them at room temperature, covered, until the morning. Then you will walk into the kitchen knowing that a fresh treat awaits you to start your day.

Similarly, any batter cake or pancake batter can be prepared the night before and cooked on the griddle in the morning. When was the last time you had golden-brown homemade pancakes with maple syrup? If all else fails, though, there is always Sunday morning for a special and leisurely breakfast.

Muffins, biscuits, and griddle cakes all have European antecedents, but the American versions developed early and represented a distinct departure from their predecessors. They used to great advantage the native grain products—cornmeal, hominy, rice, and buckwheat—as well as wheat flour when available. The earliest of typically American griddle cakes may have been one made of cornmeal, milk, and eggs, first set down by Amelia Simmons in *American Cookery* (1796) as "Indian Slapjacks."

I don't want to leave the impression that the recipes in this chapter are only appropriate for breakfast. On the contrary, biscuits are a part of every traditional southern meal, and muffins taste just as good at lunch. In the case of Rice Muffins, they are a superb accompaniment to soups for lunch or supper. But taken all in all, these treats are particularly suited to making our first meal of the day more enticing and less likely to fall by the wayside.

BUTTERMILK BISCUITS

Buttermilk biscuits are the standard in southern biscuits. However, there is no real standard recipe, as one cook's method can cause another cook to have fits. This recipe was handed down to a friend by her Aunt Burnace from Ellisville, Virginia. Burnace's use of oil rather than butter or shortening is a bit unorthodox, but I like the opportunity to use safflower oil instead of butter, which works very well here.

1¼ cups whole wheat flour
¾ cup unbleached white flour
2 teaspoons baking powder
½ teaspoon baking soda
1 teaspoon salt
¾ cup buttermilk
¼ cup safflower oil

Preheat the oven to 425° F.

In a mixing bowl, sift together the first 5 ingredients. Stir in the buttermilk and oil, a bit at a time, and work together to form a soft dough.

Turn the dough out onto a well-floured board. Knead for a minute or two, adding a small amount of flour if the dough is too sticky. You can make the biscuits in one of two ways: Either roll the dough out to about a ½-inch thickness and cut it with a biscuit cutter 2 inches in diameter; or just pinch the dough off in small bits, about 1½ inches in diameter, and pat into nice biscuit shapes. Place the biscuits on a lightly oiled cookie sheet. Bake for 12 to 15 minutes, or until touched with golden brown on top. Transfer the biscuits to a plate to cool.

Makes 12 to 15 biscuits

Our living consisted almost invariably of coffee, and hot short cakes, called biscuits.

—John Palmer
Journal of Travels in the U.S,
1818

POTATO BISCUITS

Here are two biscuit recipes (the second recipe follows) with a similar idea—adding a quantity of mashed potato to the dough, with white potato for the northern recipe and sweet potato for the southern. This excellent biscuit is from America's "heartland." If you'd like to try a savory variation, add some dried herbs to the dough.

1½ cups whole wheat flour
1½ teaspoons baking powder
½ teaspoon salt
2½ tablespoons butter
1 medium potato, cooked, peeled,
    and well mashed (about 1 cup)
About ½ cup whole or low-fat milk

Preheat the oven to 400° F.

In a mixing bowl, sift together the flour, baking powder, and salt. Work the butter in with the tines of a fork until the mixture resembles a coarse meal. Work in the mashed potato and enough milk to form a soft dough.

Turn the dough out onto a well-floured board. Knead for 2 to 3 minutes, adding a small amount of flour if the dough is too sticky. Divide the dough into 12 parts and shape into balls. Arrange on a lightly oiled cookie sheet and pat down a bit to flatten. Bake for 20 minutes, or until the tops are golden and a toothpick inserted into the center of one tests clean. Transfer the biscuits to a plate to cool.

Makes 12 biscuits

SWEET POTATO BISCUITS

In today's restaurants, North or South, travelers are apt to be served biscuits that are more often than not made from a chalky mix. Thus, I was especially glad to have been able to enjoy these subtly sweet, traditional biscuits while visiting Virginia's Colonial Williamsburg.

1¼ cups whole wheat flour
½ cup unbleached white flour
2 teaspoons baking powder
½ teaspoon salt
3 tablespoons butter
⅓ cup whole or low-fat milk
1 cup smoothly mashed sweet potato
3 tablespoons honey
⅓ cup finely chopped walnuts or
    pecans

Preheat the oven to 425° F.

In a mixing bowl, sift together the flours, baking powder, and salt. Work the butter in with the tines of a fork until the mixture resembles a coarse meal. Add the milk and sweet potato and work them in to form a soft dough.

Turn the dough out onto a well-floured board and knead for 2 to 3 minutes, adding a small amount of flour if the dough is too sticky. With floured hands, divide the dough into 12 equal parts. Shape into small balls and arrange on a lightly oiled cookie sheet, patting them down a bit to flatten. Bake for 15 minutes, or until a toothpick inserted into the center of one tests clean. Transfer the biscuits to a plate to cool.

Makes 12 biscuits

RICE MUFFINS

In South Carolina and Louisiana, the abundance of rice inspired cooks to use it as an ingredient in all manner of baked goods. Here is an adaptation of Rice Muffins from an old Louisiana recipe. Serve these warm—they're delicious with butter or jam for breakfast, or just plain to accompany soup for lunch or supper.

1 cup whole wheat flour
½ cup unbleached white flour
1¼ teaspoons baking powder
1 teaspoon salt
2 eggs, well beaten
1 cup whole or low-fat milk
1 cup cold, well-cooked brown rice
2 tablespoons butter, melted

Preheat the oven to 400° F.

In a mixing bowl, sift together the flours, baking powder, and salt. In another bowl, beat together the eggs, milk, rice, and melted butter. Gradually add the wet ingredients to the dry and stir together vigorously until thoroughly blended. Divide the batter evenly among the 12 cups of a well-oiled muffin tin. Bake for 25 to 30 minutes, or until the muffins are lightly browned and a toothpick inserted into the center of one tests clean. When the muffins are cool enough to handle, transfer them to a plate or rack to cool.

Makes 12 muffins

HOMINY MUFFINS

Making muffins of cooked grits was a common practice in the nineteenth century and was not confined to southern cooks. The grits give these muffins a nice, moist texture.

1 cup water
¼ cup (scant) regular or quick grits
1 tablespoon butter
2 eggs, well beaten
1 cup whole or low-fat milk
2 teaspoons honey
1½ cups whole wheat flour
1¼ teaspoons baking powder
½ teaspoon salt

Preheat the oven to 350° F.

Bring the water to a rolling boil in a heavy saucepan. Pour in the grits, in a thin steady stream, stirring them carefully to avoid lumping. Cook over very low heat until done, about 25 minutes for regular grits or 3 to 4 minutes for quick grits. Remove from the heat and stir in the butter to melt.

In a mixing bowl, combine the cooked grits with the eggs, milk, and honey and stir together until well blended. Add the flour, baking powder, and salt and beat together until thoroughly combined.

Divide the batter evenly among the 12 cups of an oiled muffin tin. Bake for 25 minutes, or until the tops are golden. When the muffins are cool enough to handle, transfer them to a plate or rack to cool.

Makes 12 muffins

APPLE MUFFINS

Inspired by old recipes from both New England and America's "heartland," these chewy muffins make a delightful change-of-pace treat for breakfast.

1 egg, well beaten
¼ cup packed light brown sugar
2 tablespoons butter, melted, or
  safflower oil
1 cup whole or low-fat milk
1¼ cups whole wheat flour
½ cup unbleached white flour
2 teaspoons baking powder
½ teaspoon cinnamon
¼ teaspoon ground cloves
¼ cup wheat germ
½ teaspoon salt
1 cup peeled, finely diced apple
  (about 1 medium)
½ cup raisins

The servant will bring you hot muffins and corn battercakes every 2 minutes.

—*Maryland Historical Magazine,*
  1833

Preheat the oven to 350° F.

In a mixing bowl, combine the beaten egg with the sugar until it dissolves. Add the melted butter or oil and the milk and beat together until smooth.

In another mixing bowl, sift together the flours, baking powder, and spices. Stir in the wheat germ and salt. Add the wet ingredients gradually to the dry and beat vigorously to form a smooth, stiff batter. Stir in the diced apple and raisins.

Divide the batter evenly among the 12 cups of an oiled muffin tin. Bake for 25 to 30 minutes, or until the muffins are golden and a toothpick inserted into the center of one tests clean. When the muffins are cool enough to handle, transfer them to a plate or rack to cool.

Makes 12 muffins

BASIC BUTTERMILK PANCAKES

Pancakes have been an American tradition since early colonial times. The earliest of American cookbooks refer to them as flapjacks, and over the many years, dozens of varieties have developed. This basic recipe can certainly be used on its own or as a jumping-off point for the recipes that follow, which fill the pancakes with good things.

1 cup whole wheat flour
½ cup unbleached white flour
1 teaspoon baking powder
½ teaspoon baking soda
1 egg, beaten
2 cups buttermilk
Maple syrup or jam

In a mixing bowl, sift together the flours, baking powder, and soda. Make a well in the center and place in it the beaten egg and the buttermilk. Stir vigorously with a whisk until the batter is smooth. Drop the batter onto a moderately hot nonstick griddle or a large, nonstick Silverstone skillet in amounts enough to form thin cakes approximately 4 inches in diameter. Cook on both sides until golden brown. Serve hot with maple syrup or jam.

Makes 12 to 15 pancakes

VARIATION:

For New England Currant Pancakes, simply add ½ cup lightly floured currants and ½ teaspoon cinnamon to the basic buttermilk batter. Cook as directed above.

Women are going wild over the pancake hat.

—*Kansas City Times,*
September 1931

BANANA-PECAN PANCAKES

I first had these fabulous pancakes at the Coffee Pot restaurant in New Orleans, making for a very memorable breakfast in their charming, antiquated courtyard. I later discovered that they are fairly common not only in that area but also in the Southwest, where I enjoyed them again.

1 recipe Basic Buttermilk Pancakes
   (page 22)
2 large bananas, thinly sliced
⅔ cup coarsely chopped pecans
½ teaspoon cinnamon
Maple syrup or jam

Prepare the batter as directed for Basic Buttermilk Pancakes. Fold in the bananas, pecans, and cinnamon. Cook as directed in the recipe and serve hot with maple syrup or jam.

Makes 18 to 22 pancakes

MAINE RYE PANCAKES

This isn't a common recipe, but an interesting old one from New England. The combination of flours make for a filling and hearty breakfast.

¾ cup rye flour
½ cup whole wheat flour
¼ cup unbleached white flour
1 teaspoon baking powder
½ teaspoon baking soda
2 cups buttermilk
2 tablespoons molasses
Maple syrup

Sift together into a mixing bowl the first 5 ingredients. Add the buttermilk and molasses and beat together until smoothly blended. Drop the batter onto a moderately hot nonstick griddle or a large, nonstick Silverstone skillet in amounts to form thin, 3- to 4-inch pancakes. Cook on both sides until golden brown. Serve hot with maple syrup.

Makes 12 to 15 pancakes

BUCKWHEAT CAKES

Buckwheat cakes were well-loved in the late nineteenth century, so much so that an English traveler said in 1870, "It is hard for the American to rise from his winter breakfast without his buckwheat cakes." I was delighted, yet very much surprised, that one could still get good buckwheat cakes for breakfast in the South. These pancakes are wholesome and filling and even *look* healthy. Since yeast is involved in the process, you must begin making them the night before.

1 cup whole or low-fat milk
1¼ cups lukewarm water
½ package active dry yeast
1½ cups buckwheat flour
½ cup whole wheat flour
1 tablespoon molasses
½ teaspoon salt
½ teaspoon baking soda
Maple syrup

Scald the milk by bringing it to just under the boiling point. Combine it with the lukewarm water in a mixing bowl and allow the mixture to cool to lukewarm. Sprinkle the yeast into the lukewarm mixture and let it stand for 10 minutes to dissolve.

In another bowl, combine the flours. Gradually add the wet mixture to the dry and beat until smooth. Cover and let stand at room temperature overnight.

In the morning, whisk in the molasses, salt, and baking soda. Ladle enough batter onto a moderately hot nonstick griddle to form thin cakes about 3 to 4 inches in diameter. Cook until nicely browned on both sides. Serve hot with maple syrup.

Makes 16 to 20 pancakes

James Whistler, the noted American painter, was such a great fan of buckwheat cakes that he introduced them to London society. Perhaps it was his well-known mother, a fine cook, who introduced them to her son.

LACE-EDGED CORNMEAL BATTER CAKES

Breakfast cakes of cornmeal are an old southern home cooking tradition, and I, who had never before had anything like this, have learned to love the contrast of the flavors of crisp cornmeal and maple syrup. These are so named because when your griddle is really hot, bubbles burst on the edges of the cakes, thus forming a "lacy" effect.

1 cup cornmeal
1 cup boiling water
¼ cup whole wheat flour
½ teaspoon salt
1 teaspoon baking powder
1 egg
1 cup whole or low-fat milk
Butter for frying
Maple syrup or honey

Place the cornmeal in an ovenproof bowl and pour the boiling water over it. Let it stand for 10 minutes.

Combine the cornmeal with the flour, salt, baking powder, egg, and milk in the container of a food processor or blender. Process until completely smooth.

Heat just enough butter to coat the bottom of a nonstick griddle or a large nonstick Silverstone skillet. Ladle on enough batter to form thin, 3-inch cakes. Cook until golden brown and crisp on both sides. Serve hot with maple syrup or honey.

Makes 12 to 15 batter cakes

RICE AND CORNMEAL BATTER CAKES

These wholesome griddle cakes, from a common old southern recipe, make an uncommonly hearty and delicious breakfast.

½ cup cornmeal
½ cup whole wheat flour
½ teaspoon baking soda
¼ teaspoon salt
1 cup well-cooked brown rice
2 eggs, well beaten
1 cup buttermilk
Butter for frying
Maple syrup or honey

In a mixing bowl, combine the cornmeal, flour, soda, and salt. Stir in the rice until it is evenly distributed within the meal, then add the eggs and buttermilk and stir vigorously until the mixture is well blended.

Heat just enough butter to coat the bottom of a nonstick griddle or a large nonstick Silverstone skillet. Ladle on enough batter to from thin, 3- to 4-inch cakes. Cook on both sides until nicely browned. Serve hot with maple syrup or honey.

Makes 16 to 18 batter cakes

Chapter 2
LOAF BREADS AND PAN BREADS

I was so exceedingly surprised at seeing on the table a great variety of beautiful-looking bread, made both from fine wheaten flour and Indian corn, that I exclaimed, "Bless me, we must be in Virginia!"

—George Featherstonhaugh
  English traveler in the United States, 1834

WE MUST BE IN... VIRGINIA

★ Sally Lunn Bread

★ Buttermilk Corn Bread

★ Anadama Bread

★ Molasses Cornbread

★ Spoonbread

The search for great regional breads rewarded me with plenty of fine basic ones as well as a number with some offbeat twists that gave them their uniquely American character. Southern breads containing rice or squash; Shaker breads with potatoes, herbs, and cheese; and a "Tex-Mex" corn bread filled with the ubiquitous hot chile are among those that proved delightfully different.

Like so many other categories of American cooking, breadmaking has its roots firmly planted in the knowledge of corn that the Indians passed along to the colonists. Thus, cornmeal was known well into the nineteenth century as Indian meal. The preference for corn breads in early days was as much a matter of practicality as taste. Besides its being a hardier crop than wheat, it was better suited to being ground by the crude millstones used then. In addition, the yeasting process required for wheat breads was tedious, and homemade baking powders weren't always reliable. As time went on, wheat breads grew in popularity in the colonies but were still mixed with a portion of cornmeal, as in the case of the delicious Anadama Bread.

At Colonial Williamsburg, the old method of grinding corn between two stones, powered by a windmill, was demonstrated to me by Cornelius Black, a descendant of several generations of Virginia millers. The rather coarse, uneven meal he produces is similar to that produced before the 1850s. Maria Parloa, in *Miss Parloa's Kitchen Companion* (1887), writes longingly of the coarser meal, commenting that though it didn't keep as well due to its high moisture content, it produced a sweet and delicious flavor. She goes on to complain that as the corn was dried quicker at high temperatures and ground ever finer, "these changes in the meal have damaged it considerably and it is almost impossible to get the moist, sweet corn-bread of years gone by." This might explain why the corn breads that came out best for me were those that contained plenty of "moisturizers"—molasses, cheese, and lots of buttermilk.

Whole wheat flour in the nineteenth century was a bran-filled meal called Graham flour, after the eccentric clergyman and health advocate, Sylvester Graham. But, as Karen Hess comments in her annotations to Mary Randolph's *Virginia Housewife* (1824), it's safe to venture that even the general flour was not as finely bolted as it is today and must have contained a portion of the healthy germ and bran.

After learning to make the breads in this chapter, I was finally freed of the fear of making leavened breads. The extra time and effort were well rewarded by the sight of golden loaves bursting from their tins and the aroma of fresh bread in the house. For those of you who are *really* too busy for yeasted breads, there will be several very satisfying and unusual quick breads to choose from as well.

BUTTERMILK CORN BREAD

It's hard to think of a more classic American bread than corn bread. Almost all corn breads, and there are many varieties, can be traced back to the American Indians—cornmeal, as previously mentioned, was called Indian meal well into the nineteenth century. Buttermilk-Corn Bread is common to the South and to New England.

1½ cups cornmeal
½ cup whole wheat flour
2 teaspoons baking powder
1 teaspoon baking soda
1 teaspoon salt
2 eggs, well beaten
3 tablespoons light brown sugar
1¾ cups buttermilk
2 tablespoons butter, melted

Preheat the oven to 425° F.

Sift together the first 5 ingredients into a mixing bowl. In another bowl, beat the eggs together with the sugar, buttermilk, and melted butter. Stir the wet ingredients into the dry and stir vigorously to blend into a smooth batter. Pour the mixture into a well-oiled, shallow 9-by-9-inch aluminum pan.

Bake for 20 to 25 minutes, or until the edges turn golden and a knife inserted into the center tests clean. Allow the bread to cool in the pan and cut into 9 or 12 squares to serve.

MOLASSES CORN BREAD

Here is an Old South variety of corn bread. Combine it with a piece of sharp Cheddar cheese and some fresh fruit for a pleasant lunch.

1 cup cornmeal
½ cup whole wheat flour
½ cup unbleached white flour
2 teaspoons baking powder
1 teaspoon salt
1 egg, well beaten
1 cup low-fat milk
¼ cup molasses
2 tablespoons butter, melted

Preheat the oven to 400° F.

Sift together the first 5 ingredients into a mixing bowl. In another bowl, combine the beaten egg with the milk, molasses, and melted butter. Beat together until well mixed. Add the wet ingredients to the dry and stir together vigorously until thoroughly combined. Pour the mixture into an oiled, shallow 9-by-9-inch aluminum pan.

Bake for 20 to 25 minutes, or until a knife inserted into the center tests clean. Allow the bread to cool in the pan and cut into 9 or 12 squares to serve.

GREEN CHILE CORN BREAD

This is the Texas and Southwest version of corn bread, a more contemporary recipe than the previous two, and still a very popular one. For real chile-heads, make this with the jalapeños to produce an incendiary bread. For those of you who are wary of breads that must be eaten with a fire extinguisher, do use the mild chiles. Either way, this is a rich and unusually tasty treat.

1½ cups cornmeal
½ cup whole wheat flour
1½ teaspoons baking soda
1 teaspoon baking powder
1 teaspoon salt
½ cup sour cream
2 eggs, well beaten
1 cup buttermilk
1 cup grated Cheddar cheese
2 jalapeño peppers, seeded and
 minced, or one 4-ounce can mild
 green chiles, drained and
 chopped
½ cup cooked fresh corn kernels
 (optional)
2 tablespoons butter, melted

The North thinks it knows how to make corn bread, but this is mere superstition.

—Mark Twain

Preheat the oven to 400° F.

Sift together the first 5 ingredients into a mixing bowl. In another bowl, beat the sour cream into the eggs and gradually stir in the buttermilk. Add the wet mixture to the dry and stir together vigorously until well blended.

Stir in the grated cheese, jalapeños or chiles, and optional corn kernels. Pour the melted butter into a shallow 9-by-9-inch aluminum pan and swirl it around until it coats the bottom and sides. Pour the excess butter into the batter and stir it in. Pour the batter into the pan.

Bake for 20 to 25 minutes, or until the top is golden and a knife inserted into the center tests clean. Allow the bread to cool in the pan and cut into 9 or 12 squares to serve.

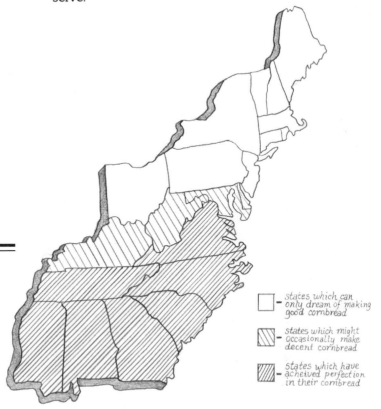

- states which can only dream of making good cornbread
- states which might occasionally make decent cornbread
- states which have acheived perfection in their cornbread

ANADAMA BREAD

One of the earliest of colonial American breads, Anadama Bread is also one of the finest. Its outstanding texture and flavor put it high on my list of favorites.

1 cup whole or low-fat milk
1 cup boiling water
½ cup cornmeal
2 tablespoons butter, cut into bits
1 teaspoon salt
¼ cup molasses
1 package active dry yeast
½ cup lukewarm water
3 cups whole wheat flour
1½ to 2 cups unbleached white flour

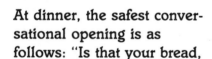

At dinner, the safest conversational opening is as follows: "Is that your bread, or mine?"

—Francis W. Crowninshield
Manners for the Metropolis, 1909

In a large, heavy saucepan, scald the milk by heating it to just below the boiling point over moderate heat. Add to it the boiling water. Very slowly, in a steady stream, pour in the cornmeal, whisking it in quickly to avoid lumping. Stir in the butter until it melts, then add the salt and molasses and mix well. Let the mixture cool to lukewarm.

Dissolve the yeast in the lukewarm water. Let it stand for 10 minutes, then stir gently. Pour it into the lukewarm milk-and-cornmeal mixture. Work the flours in, a cup or so at a time, then turn the dough out onto a well-floured board. Knead for 8 to 10 minutes, or until the dough is smooth and elastic, adding a bit more flour if necessary so that it loses its stickiness. Form the dough into a smooth round and set it in a floured bowl. Cover with a clean tea towel and let it rise in a warm place until doubled in bulk, about 1½ hours.

Punch the dough down, knead briefly, and divide in two parts. Shape into loaves and place them in oiled 9-by-5-by-3-inch aluminum loaf pans. Let the dough rise again, covered and in a warm place until doubled in bulk, about 1 hour.

Bake in a preheated 350° F oven for 45 to 50 minutes, or until the loaves sound hollow when tapped and are nicely browned. When the loaves are cool enough to handle, remove them from their pans and allow them to cool on a rack.

Makes two loaves

SALLY LUNN BREAD

A bread with a strange name and a complicated history, this is another early colonial bread. The absence of any cornmeal might suggest that its use was more prevalent with the "upper crust," so to speak, since wheat flour was a more valuable commodity. The recipe is thought to have perhaps originated in England as a bun. By the time it reached the United States, its popularity was mainly as a tea bread and it was often baked like a brioche, in a "Turk's-head" mold. Sally Lunn recipes have been included in dozens of cookbooks from the early nineteenth to the mid-twentieth century, with all manner of additions and strange explanations for the name. This recipe is adapted from the one considered to be the classic, from Eliza Leslie's immensely popular mid-nineteenth-century cookbook, *Directions for Cookery*. She states simply that, "This cake is named after the inventress." This is a lovely and very light bread.

1 cup whole or low-fat milk
¼ cup (½ stick) butter, cut into bits
1 package active dry yeast
¼ cup lukewarm water
2 cups whole wheat flour
2 cups unbleached white flour
1 teaspoon salt
2 eggs, very well beaten

In a small saucepan, scald the milk by bringing it to just below the boiling point. Let it cool for 5 minutes, then add to it the butter. Allow the milk to cool to lukewarm.

Dissolve the yeast in the lukewarm water. Let it stand for 10 minutes, then stir gently. Add this to the lukewarm milk mixture.

Sift together the flours and salt into a mixing bowl. Make a well in the center and put into it the well-beaten eggs followed by the wet mixture. Beat together vigorously with a wooden spoon until thoroughly blended. The dough should have the texture of a very heavy batter and will be sticky. Shape it into a fairly smooth round and place it in a very-well-floured bowl. Cover with a clean tea towel and let it rise in a warm place until doubled in bulk, about 1½ hours.

With well-floured hands (the dough will still be sticky), punch the dough down. Turn it out, with the aid of a cake spatula, onto a well-floured board. Arrange the dough in an oiled 10-inch tube pan or divide it in half and place it in two small oiled loaf pans. Let the dough rise again, covered and in a warm place, until doubled in bulk, about 1 hour.

Bake in a preheated 350° F oven for 45 to 50 minutes, or until the tops are golden brown and the bread sounds hollow when tapped. When the loaves are cool enough to handle, remove them from their pans and allow them to cool on a rack.

Makes one 10-inch tube loaf or two small loaves

CAROLINA RICE AND WHEAT BREAD

Rice was a staple crop in South Carolina early in the state's history and, like the corn of other locales, worked its way into nearly every category of cooking and baking. Thus, the addition of rice or rice flour to breads is a very early practice that originated in this region. This hearty bread is adapted from Sarah Rutledge's *The Carolina Housewife* (1847), which contained numerous recipes for breads that combined rice with wheat. It's a delicious and healthful idea that I hope will be revived.

½ cup raw brown rice
2 cups water
1 cup low-fat milk, scalded
¼ cup (½ stick) butter, cut into bits
2 tablespoons molasses
1 package active dry yeast
¼ cup lukewarm water
3½ cups whole wheat flour
1½ cups unbleached white flour
1½ teaspoons salt

Cook the rice in the 2 cups water until all the water is absorbed (this four-to-one ratio will cook the rice to a softer-than-usual texture).

Scald the milk by heating it to just under the boiling point. Remove from the heat and place in it the bits of butter. Add the molasses and let the mixture stand until it is lukewarm.

Dissolve the yeast in the lukewarm water. Let it stand for 10 minutes, then stir it gently. Add it to the lukewarm milk mixture and stir until well blended.

In a large mixing bowl, combine the flours and salt. Pour in the milk mixture, a bit at a time, and work it in until the flour is completely moistened. Add the cooked rice and work it in with your hands until the dough holds together.

Turn the dough out onto a well-floured board and knead for 10 to 12 minutes. This dough will require some diligent working before it becomes elastic, due to the heaviness of the rice. Pat the dough into a smooth round and place it in a floured bowl. Cover with a clean tea towel and let the dough rise in a warm place until doubled in bulk, about 1½ hours.

Punch the dough down, divide it in half and shape into loaves. Place them in oiled 9-by-5-by-3-inch loaf pans and allow them to rise until doubled again, covered and in a warm place about 1 to 1½ hours.

Bake in a preheated 350° F oven for 45 to 50 minutes, or until the tops of the loaves are lightly browned and sound hollow when tapped. When the loaves are cool enough to handle, remove them from their pans and allow them to cool on a rack.

Makes 2 loaves

PHILPY (Hot Rice Bread)

This is an old South Carolina recipe, the origin of whose name is obscure. The first recorded recipe may be that in *The Carolina Housewife* (1847), attributed to Sarah Rutledge. Don't be deterred by the simplicity of it—it's absolutely delicious. I love it for breakfast with maple syrup.

1 cup well-cooked brown rice
1 egg, well beaten
½ cup whole or low-fat milk
⅓ cup whole wheat flour
½ teaspoon salt
½ teaspoon baking powder
2 tablespoons butter, melted
Butter, jam, or maple syrup

Preheat the oven to 400° F.

Mash the rice as finely as possible with the tines of a fork. In a mixing bowl, combine the beaten egg with the milk, then stir in the mashed rice. Add the flour, salt, and baking powder and stir briskly until the mixture is smooth. Stir in the melted butter. Pour the mixture into an oiled 9-inch pie pan.

Bake for 30 minutes, or until golden brown and set. Cut into wedges and serve hot with butter, jam, or maple syrup.

Serves 4 to 6

Q. My husband buys forty-five cents worth of mixed drinks every time I send him for a five-cent loaf of bread. How long will we keep our home?
A. It takes longer to drink up some homes than it does others. Try baking your own bread.

—Kin Hubbard
Abe Martin's Almanack, 1911

OLD-FASHIONED OAT BREAD

Breads containing rolled oats were once common in New England and in the Great Plains states, such as Nebraska. The oats all but disappear during the baking process, but leave a subtly chewy texture to this hearty bread.

1½ cups rolled oats
3 tablespoons butter, cut into bits
1 cup whole or low-fat milk
1 cup boiling water
1 package active dry yeast
¼ cup lukewarm water
⅓ cup molasses
3 cups whole wheat flour
1½ cups unbleached white flour
1½ teaspoons salt

Combine the oats with the butter in a large mixing bowl. In a small saucepan, scald the milk by bringing it to just under the boiling point. Pour both the scalded milk and the boiling water over the oats and stir to melt the butter. Let the mixture cool to lukewarm.

Pour the yeast into the lukewarm water and let it stand for 10 minutes to dissolve. Add it along with the molasses to the oats mixture and stir together gently.

In another mixing bowl, combine the flours and salt. Work the flour mixture into the oats mixture, a bit at a time, ending by using floured hands. When the dough holds together, turn it out onto a floured board and knead for about 7 minutes. Add small amounts of flour until the dough loses its stickiness. Pat into a smooth round and place the dough in a floured bowl. Cover with a clean tea towel and set in a warm place to rise until doubled in bulk, about 1½ hours.

Punch the dough down and knead on a floured board for 5 minutes, or until it is quite elastic. Divide the dough in half, shape into loaves, and place them in oiled 9-by-5-by-3-inch aluminum loaf pans. Let the loaves rise for 1 hour, covered and in a warm place or until doubled in bulk again.

Bake in a preheated 350° F oven for 45 to 55 minutes, or until the tops are nicely browned and the loaves feel hollow when tapped. When the loaves are cool enough to handle, remove them from their pans and allow them to cool on a rack.

Makes 2 loaves

ZUNI QUICK BREAD

There are several types of Zuni Bread from different parts of the Southwest. What they have in common is that they're all hearty breads with both wheat flour and cornmeal. I chose to adapt this quick version because I liked the idea of including sunflower seeds.

1½ cups whole wheat flour
¼ cup unbleached white flour
⅓ cup cornmeal
2½ teaspoons baking powder
½ teaspoon baking soda
1 teaspoon salt
2 eggs, well beaten
1 cup buttermilk
3 tablespoons molasses
2 tablespoons safflower oil
⅓ cup toasted sunflower seeds

[The Indians] make their Bread of the Indian corn, wild Oats, or the Seed of the Sunflower.

—Robert Beverly
The History and Present State of Virginia, 1705

Preheat the oven to 350° F.

Sift together the first 6 ingredients into a mixing bowl. In another bowl, combine the beaten eggs with the buttermilk, molasses, and oil and beat together until well blended. Add the wet ingredients to the dry and beat together vigorously to form a stiff batter. Stir in the sunflower seeds. Pour the mixture into an oiled 9-by-5-by-3-inch aluminum loaf pan.

Bake for 45 to 50 minutes, or until the top is nicely browned and a knife inserted into the center tests clean. When the loaf is cool enough to handle, remove it from its pan and allow it to cool on a rack.

Makes 1 loaf

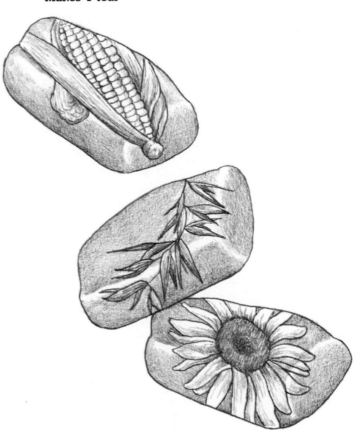

SHAKER HERB BREAD

Shaker cookery in America is perhaps best known for having been far ahead of its time in its creative use of culinary herbs. An old Shaker journal extols their merits by stating that "they stimulate appetite, they give character to food and add charm and variety to ordinary dishes." Herbs even found their way into the Shakers' marvelous breads. Presented here are two of the best-known examples.

1 cup whole or low-fat milk
3 tablespoons butter, cut into bits
1 cup lukewarm water
3 tablespoons honey
1 package active dry yeast
4 cups whole wheat flour
1 cup unbleached white flour
2 teaspoons dried dill
½ teaspoon dried thyme
½ teaspoon dried marjoram
2 teaspoons caraway seeds
1½ teaspoons salt

Scald the milk by bringing it to just under the boiling point. In a large mixing bowl, combine it with the butter, lukewarm water, and honey. Allow to cool to lukewarm, then sprinkle in the yeast and let it stand for 10 minutes to dissolve. Stir the mixture gently.

In another bowl, combine the flours, herbs, and salt. Work this mixture into the wet mixture to form a soft dough. Turn the dough out onto a well-floured board and knead for about 8 minutes, adding additional flour until the dough loses most of its stickiness. Pat into a smooth round and place in a floured bowl. Cover with a clean tea towel and set in a warm place to rise until doubled in bulk, about 1½ hours.

Punch the dough down, then turn out onto a floured board and knead for a minute or two. Divide the dough in half and shape into loaves. Place them in oiled 9-by-5-by-3-inch aluminum loaf pans. Cover and let them rise in a warm place until doubled in bulk again, about 1 hour.

Bake in a preheated 350° F oven for 45 to 50 minutes, or until the loaves are nicely browned and sound hollow when tapped. When the loaves are cool enough to handle, remove them from their pans and allow them to cool on a rack.

Makes 2 loaves

POTATO-DILL BREAD

Another great Shaker bread utilizing their special touch with herbs, this has become one of my favorites. It has a wonderful texture—very light and springy. Fresh dill is preferable, but you have the option of using it dried if you must.

1 large potato, cooked, peeled, and
    well mashed (about 1½ cups)
1 cup warm water
1 package active dry yeast
¼ cup lukewarm water
¼ cup (½ stick) butter, softened
2 tablespoons light brown sugar
3 tablespoons minced fresh dill or 1
    tablespoon dried dill
3½ cups whole wheat flour
1 cup unbleached white flour
1½ teaspoons salt
Dill seed for topping (optional)

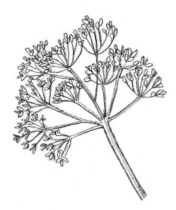

Combine the mashed potatoes with the warm water in a bowl and stir until well blended. Dissolve the yeast in the ¼ cup lukewarm water. Let it stand for 10 minutes, then stir gently.

In the meantime, cream the butter and sugar together in a large mixing bowl until light and fluffy. Slowly add the potato mixture, beating vigorously to combine. Stir in the dissolved yeast and the dill.

Combine the flours and salt, then stir the flour mixture, about a cup at a time, into the wet mixture. Once all the flour is in, work everything together with floured hands. Turn the mixture out onto a well-floured board. Knead for about 8 minutes, adding additional flour only as needed to form a light, elastic dough.

Pat the dough into a smooth round and place it in a floured bowl. Cover with a clean tea towel and let it rise in a warm place until doubled in bulk, about 1½ hours.

Punch the dough down, then divide it in half and shape into loaves. Place them in oiled 9-by-5-by-3-inch aluminum loaf pans. Cover and let the loaves rise in a warm place until doubled in bulk again, about 1 hour. Sprinkle with the optional dill seed.

Bake in a preheated 350° F oven for 45 to 50 minutes, or until the tops are golden brown and feel hollow when tapped. When the loaves are cool enough to handle, remove them from their pans and allow them to cool on a rack.

Makes 2 loaves

SHAKER CHEDDAR BREAD

The favored cheese of New England is used to great advantage in this delicious quick bread, from the archives of the Shakers of New Hampshire. Practically a cheese sandwich with the cheese built right in, this bread makes for a great brown-bag or picnic lunch with a salad and fresh fruit. It's also a perfect protein complement to hearty bean soups, such as Black Bean Soup (page 47).

1½ cups whole wheat flour
½ cup unbleached white flour
2 teaspoons baking powder
1 teaspoon salt
¼ cup (½ stick) unsalted butter, softened
1½ cups firmly packed grated sharp Cheddar cheese
2 eggs, well beaten
1 cup low-fat milk
1 tablespoon honey
1 teaspoon dried dill (optional)

At family dinners, where the common household bread is used, it should never be cut less than an inch and a half thick. There is nothing more plebian than *thin* bread at dinner.

—Charles Day
Hints on Etiquette, 1843

Preheat the oven to 350° F.

Sift the flours, baking powder, and salt together into a large mixing bowl. Cut the butter into 4 or 5 bits. Blend it into the flour mixture by pressing it in with the tines of a fork until the mixture resembles a coarse meal. Stir in the grated cheese.

In another bowl, combine the beaten eggs with the milk, honey, and optional dill. Beat together until well blended. Add the wet mixture to the dry and beat together vigorously until thoroughly mixed. Pour the mixture into an oiled 9-by-5-by-3-inch aluminum loaf pan.

Bake for about 50 minutes, or until the top is nicely browned and a knife inserted into the center tests clean. When the loaf is cool enough to handle, remove it from its pan and allow it to cool on a rack.

Makes 1 loaf

Note: This bread freezes beautifully, so you might like to double the recipe and make one loaf to use fresh and one to freeze for later use.

It is not proper to shock your guests by serving them thin bread at dinner.

GOLDEN SQUASH OR PUMPKIN BREAD

The abundant squash crop of the Indians worked its way into every category of cookery, whether soups, desserts, or even breads. This moist and just slightly sweet quick bread is a contemporary interpretation of a traditional idea.

1½ cups whole wheat flour
½ cup unbleached white flour
2 teaspoons baking powder
½ teaspoon salt
1 teaspoon cinnamon
¼ teaspoon ground cloves
¼ teaspoon ground allspice
¼ cup wheat germ
2 eggs, well beaten
3 tablespoons safflower oil
⅓ cup fresh orange juice
¼ cup packed light brown sugar
1 cup well-pureed cooked butternut
   squash or pumpkin
⅔ cup chopped pecans or walnuts

New Haven is celebrated for having given the name of "pumpkin-heads" to all New Englanders. It originated from the "Blue Laws," which enjoined every male to have his hair cut round by a cap. When caps were not to be had, they substituted the hard shell of a pumpkin, which being put on the head every Saturday, the hair is cut by the shell all round the head.

—The Rev. Samuel Peters
General History of Connecticut, 1877

Preheat the oven to 350° F.

Sift together the flours, baking powder, salt, and spices into a mixing bowl. Stir in the wheat germ. In another mixing bowl, beat the eggs together with the oil, orange juice, and sugar, stirring until the sugar dissolves. Add the squash or pumpkin puree and beat together until smooth. Gradually add the wet ingredients to the dry and beat together vigorously until thoroughly blended. Stir in the nuts. Pour the mixture into an oiled 9-by-5-by-3-inch aluminum loaf pan.

Bake for 45 to 55 minutes, or until the top is golden brown and a knife inserted into the center tests clean. When the loaf is cool enough to handle, remove it from its pan and allow it to cool on a rack.

Makes 1 loaf

SOUTHERN SPOONBREAD

Spoonbread is one of the most characteristic dishes of traditional southern cooking. Really a cross between a pan bread and a soufflé, it is probably so named because you can scoop it out of its pan—or eat it—with a spoon. Here is the recipe at its most basic. Although it is delicious in this simple form, you might like to try adding to it bits of sautéed green or red bell pepper, onion, zucchini, or cooked corn kernels.

2 cups water
1 cup cornmeal
1 teaspoon salt
2 tablespoons butter, cut into bits
1 cup whole or low-fat milk
3 eggs, separated, at room
    temperature

Preheat the oven to 375° F.

Bring the water to a boil in a heavy saucepan or double boiler. Slowly, pour in the cornmeal in a thin, steady stream, whisking it to avoid lumping. Add the salt and cook, covered, over very low heat for 20 minutes, stirring occasionally. Remove from the heat.

Stir the butter into the cooked cornmeal until it melts. Add the milk, half at a time, followed by the egg yolks, and stir until well blended. If you choose to use any additional ingredients, such as the vegetables mentioned above, add them at this point.

Beat the egg whites until they form stiff peaks. Fold them gently into the batter, then pour the batter into a well-oiled 1½-quart casserole or soufflé dish. Bake for 30 to 35 minutes, or until the top is golden and the spoonbread is set. Serve at once. Any leftover spoonbread may be cut into squares once it is chilled and sautéed on all sides in a little butter until the outside is lightly browned and crisp.

Serves 6 to 8

Anybody that ever ate spoonbread, corn cakes or pones below Mason and Dixon's line knows that white corn is for folk and yellow for critters.

—*Christian Science Monitor*, 1944

Folks seem to love posing with white corn.

RICE AND CORNMEAL SPOONBREAD

Rice and cornmeal, with their complementary mild flavors, were often combined in old South Carolina and Louisiana recipes such as this variation of the basic spoonbread. Consider the same vegetable variations I suggested for Southern Spoonbread on the previous page. Sautéed bell pepper is especially nice.

1½ cups water
½ cup cornmeal
1 teaspoon salt
2½ tablespoons butter, cut into bits
1 cup whole or low-fat milk
2 eggs, separated, at room
    temperature.
2 cups well-cooked brown rice

Preheat the oven to 375° F.

Bring the water to a boil in a heavy saucepan or double boiler. Use the same procedure for cooking the cornmeal as described on the previous page.

Turn the cooked cornmeal out into a mixing bowl, add the butter and stir it in until it melts. Add the milk, half at a time, followed by the egg yolks and cooked rice.

Beat the egg whites until they form stiff peaks. Fold them gently into the rice-and-cornmeal mixture. Pour the mixture into a well-oiled 1½-quart casserole or soufflé dish. Bake for 30 to 35 minutes, or until the top is golden brown. Cut into squares to serve.

Serves 6

Critters find that yellow corn is perfect for tricks.

Chapter 3
SOUPS

Les vieux pots font les bonnes soupes. (It's the old pot that makes the good soup.)

—Creole proverb

Soup making, to me, is a continual source of culinary wonder and delight. I wonder, at first, how a bunch of seemingly disparate elements will come together—and then I am delighted by the way that they finally meld as a composite blend of complementary flavors and textures. Great soups have always been a backbone of American cooking, from the chowders of early New England to the thick *potages* of New Orleans. The soups that follow represent a broad cross section of regional styles, their key ingredients reading like a list of our basic native harvest: Corn, beans, rice, squash, and white and sweet potatoes are among those staples that form the basis for many of these soups. Those everyday items are transformed to outstanding savor by the ingenuity of yesterday's cooks. This inventiveness extended also to using the unexpected for the basis for more exotic soups as well—have you ever had an eggplant soup, a peanut soup, an okra soup, or a soup laced with green chiles? These offbeat finds made for a very rewarding search for soul-satisfying soups for this chapter.

My single greatest source for outstanding soups was found in the old Creole home-cooking tradition of New Orleans. Culled primarily from late-nineteenth- and early-twentieth-century Creole cookbooks, some of these soups were adapted by me to the vegetarian kitchen by simply omitting a soup bone or chicken stock from the original recipe. Others are from that variety known as Lenten soups, which were completely meatless to begin with. In either case, the Creole genius for creative seasoning made the adaptation easy, since the soups are, for that reason, already packed with flavor.

Similarly, the other soups in this chapter were chosen for their ease of adaptation, where the removal of some scraps of meat or stock would not change their intrinsic character. You will find a good selection of hearty winter soups, whose ingredients are suited to the availability of such produce in the cold months, when warming soups are most wanted. Soups for every season will be found here, whether soothing or spicy, hot or chilled, and as diverse as the origins and influences that inspired their invention.

POTAGE MAIGRE D'HIVER (Winter Fast-Day Soup)

The recipes on these two pages are old Creole Lenten soups, of which the 1901 edition of *The Picayune's Creole Cookbook* says, "The Creoles excel in preparation of soups without meat, or fast-day soups, as they are called . . . which are in great vogue during the Lenten season." These soups were apparently developed for the austere periods, when families cut down on meat consumption, but the meatless soups in the Creole cuisine are anything but austere. With their wonderful sense of herbs and spices and seasonal balance, Creole soups as well as Creole-influenced soups comprise a hefty part of this chapter. Here are a winter and a summer version of Potage Maigre, both adapted from the aforementioned edition. What they both have in common is the use of green peas—dried for winter, fresh for summer.

2 tablespoons butter
3 medium stalks celery, diced
1 large onion, chopped
2 cloves garlic, minced
7 cups water or vegetable stock
2 cups dried split peas
2 bay leaves
2 medium carrots, sliced
2 medium turnips or 1 large
   parsnip, peeled and diced
½ teaspoon dried thyme
½ teaspoon dried mint
¼ cup chopped fresh parsley
2 cups chopped fresh spinach or
   dark-green lettuce leaves
Salt and freshly ground black pepper

In a large soup pot or Dutch oven, heat the butter until it foams. Add the celery, onion, and garlic and sauté over low heat until the onion begins to turn golden. Add the water or stock, the split peas, and the bay leaves. Bring to a boil, then cover and simmer over low heat for 10 minutes. Add the carrots, turnips or parsnip, thyme, and mint. Simmer for another 45 to 50 minutes, or until the peas are mushy and the vegetables are tender. Add the spinach or lettuce and season to taste with salt and pepper. Simmer for another 15 minutes over very low heat.

If time allows, let the soup stand for an hour or so before serving. This soup thickens considerably as it stands. Add more water or stock as needed and adjust the seasonings.

Serves 8 or more

To have [peas] in perfection, they must be quite young, gathered early in the morning, kept in a cool place, and not shelled until they are ready to be dressed.

—Mary Randolph
The Virginia Housewife, 1824

POTAGE MAIGRE D'ÉTÉ (Summer Fast-Day Soup)

Here is the second of the Creole Lenten soups as described on the previous page. A light and unusual soup, it is unclear whether it originated as a Creole soup or was adopted by the region, since I saw versions of it in widespread sources, from an old Pennsylvania Dutch cookbook to the charming nineteenth-century *Whistler's Mother's Cookbook* (she called it Soup Maigre). Whatever the case, it seems as if this was not an uncommon summer soup in earlier times.

2 tablespoons butter
2 large onions, quartered and thinly sliced
1 large stalk celery, finely diced
A handful of celery leaves
1 large head romaine lettuce or 2 small heads Boston or Bibb lettuce, finely shredded
5 cups water or vegetable stock
1 egg, well beaten
1 cup steamed fresh green peas
1 cup grated, peeled and seeded cucumber
¼ cup chopped fresh parsley
Salt and freshly ground black pepper
Potato Dumplings (page 61) (optional), or sour cream or yogurt (optional)

In a large soup pot or Dutch oven, heat the butter until it foams. Add the onions and sauté over low heat until they are translucent. Add the diced celery and continue to sauté until the onions begin to turn golden. Add the celery leaves, lettuce, and water or stock. Bring to a boil, then cover and simmer for 10 to 15 minutes, or until the lettuce is wilted but still has a bit of crunch.

Stir the beaten egg into the soup in a thin, steady stream. Add the peas and grated cucumber. Adjust the consistency with a bit more water or stock if the vegetables look like they need more liquid to float in.

Season to taste with salt and lots of freshly ground pepper. Simmer over very low heat for another 10 minutes. Serve hot with Potato Dumplings if you'd like, or cold with a scoop of sour cream or yogurt.

Serves 6 to 8

RED BEAN SOUP

This thick and filling soup is an old Creole standard. It's a perfect choice for a soup-and-salad supper, teamed with a good bread and a light dessert.

1 pound dry red or kidney beans
1 medium onion, finely chopped
1 clove garlic, crushed or minced
2 bay leaves
1 tablespoon safflower oil
2 large stalks celery, diced
A handful of celery leaves, chopped
1 cup chopped ripe, juicy tomatoes
　　(substitute drained canned
　　tomatoes if necessary)
½ teaspoon dried thyme
A few grains cayenne pepper, or to
　　taste
1 tablespoon butter
1 large onion, quartered and thinly
　　sliced
3 tablespoons dry red wine or
　　sherry (optional)
Salt and freshly ground black pepper
Thinly sliced lemon for garnish

Sometimes you sow red beans, and white beans grow.

—Creole proverb akin to "the best laid plans . . ."

Rinse and sort the beans and soak them overnight in plenty of water.

The next day, drain them and place them in a large soup pot or Dutch oven in about double their volume of water along with the chopped onion, garlic, bay leaves, and safflower oil. Bring to a boil, then cover and simmer over low heat for 1½ hours. Add the celery, celery leaves, chopped tomatoes, thyme, and cayenne. Stir them in and simmer for another hour or more, or until the beans are quite tender. Remove from the heat. Discard bay leaves.

With a slotted spoon, transfer half the solid ingredients to the container of a food processor or blender and process (in batches if necessary) to a coarse puree. Stir the puree back into the soup pot.

In a small skillet, heat the butter until it foams. Add the sliced onion and sauté until it is golden brown. Stir this into the soup along with the optional wine or sherry and season to taste with salt and pepper. Return to very low heat for 10 to 15 minutes. Garnish each serving with 2 thin lemon slices.

Serves 6 to 8

BLACK BEAN SOUP

I'm very partial to black beans, so I was especially pleased to add to my repertoire this classic southern soup (with distinctive Creole overtones). The original recipes most often included some meat, such as ham, but with the robust flavor of the bean and the rather elaborate seasonings, I'm sure it will not be missed.

1 pound dried black beans
1½ tablespoons safflower oil
1 cup chopped onion
2 large carrots, chopped
2 large stalks celery, diced
2 or 3 cloves garlic, crushed or
   minced
3 tablespoons fresh parsley leaves
2 bay leaves
1 teaspoon dried basil
½ teaspoon dried thyme
¼ teaspoon ground cloves or ½
   teaspoon whole cloves
¼ teaspoon ground allspice
¼ cup dry sherry
Salt and freshly ground black pepper
1 tablespoon butter
1 large onion, quartered and sliced
Thinly sliced lemons for garnish
Finely chopped fresh parsley for
   garnish

Rinse and sort the beans, discarding withered or discolored ones. Soak overnight in plenty of water.

The next day, drain the beans and rinse them again. Place them in a large soup pot or Dutch oven with fresh water in an approximately three-to-one ratio. Bring to a boil, then cover and simmer over low heat for 1 hour. Add the oil, chopped onion, carrots, celery, garlic, and the herbs and spices. Simmer for another 1 to 1½ hours, or until the beans are soft.

With a slotted spoon, scoop out 1½ cups worth of black beans, avoiding as much as possible scooping out the other vegetables. Set aside.

Discard the bay leaves and transfer the solid ingredients, in batches, to the container of a food processor or blender. Use about ¼ cup of the cooking liquid per batch. Process until smoothly pureed, then return the puree to the soup pot along with the reserved beans. Add the sherry and season to taste with salt and pepper. Return to low heat.

In a small skillet, heat the butter until it foams. Add the sliced onion and sauté over low heat until it is nicely golden brown. Stir the sautéed onion into the soup. Simmer for 5 minutes more.

Garnish each serving with 2 round lemon slices and a bit of chopped parsley. This soup keeps very well for several days, and the flavor improves as it stands.

Serves 6 to 8

CREOLE EGGPLANT SOUP

From an old Creole recipe, this unusual soup is one of my favorite discoveries. This recipe is courtesy of the famous Commander's Palace restaurant in New Orleans, which still serves it occasionally. It is believed that the soup originated locally due to the abundance of the eggplant crop in the region.

2 tablespoons butter
1 large onion, chopped
3 medium stalks celery, diced
1 clove garlic, minced
1½ tablespoons unbleached white flour
2 large potatoes, peeled and finely diced
1 large eggplant (about 1½ pounds), peeled and finely diced
2 to 3 tablespoons chopped fresh parsley
1 tablespoon finely chopped fresh basil, or 1 teaspoon dried basil
1 teaspoon curry powder
¼ teaspoon dried thyme
1 cup whole or low-fat milk
Salt and freshly ground black pepper

Heat the butter in a large soup pot or Dutch oven until it foams. Add the onion, celery, and garlic and sauté over very low heat, stirring frequently, for 10 minutes. Add a small amount of water if the mixture begins to seem dry. Sprinkle in the flour and cook, stirring, for another minute or so.

Place the potato and eggplant dice in the soup pot along with enough water to cover all but about 1 inch of the vegetables, leaving them above the water line. Bring to a boil. At this point you should be able to push all the vegetables below the water. Stir well, then cover and simmer over low heat until the potatoes are just tender, about 15 minutes. Add the parsley, basil, and thyme and simmer another 25 minutes. Stir in the milk, more or less as needed to achieve a nice consistency, and season to taste with salt and pepper. Simmer for another 5 to 10 minutes over very low heat.

Serves 6

It is usual to commence with soup . . . when all are seated, send a plate of soup to everyone. Do not ask if they will be helped, as everyone takes it, of course.

—An American Lady
True Politeness, 1853

It is *not* correct to allow guests to wear fancy hats while eating soup.

It *is* correct to send soup to the table without asking guests if they'll be helped.

POTAGE CRÉCY (Carrot Soup)

This clove-scented Creole soup has a cheerful orange color and, if good carrots are used, a slightly sweet flavor. It's a real spirit lifter in the winter, waking up and nourishing the dulled senses.

2 tablespoons butter
2 large onions, chopped
2 cloves garlic, minced
2 medium turnips or parsnips, peeled and diced
2 medium stalks celery, diced
One 14-ounce can imported plum tomatoes with liquid, chopped
1½ pounds carrots, chopped
2½ cups water
1 teaspoon dried basil
¼ teaspoon dried thyme
3 or 4 whole cloves (preferably) or ¼ teaspoon ground cloves
1½ to 2 cups whole or low-fat milk
Salt and freshly ground black pepper
3 tablespoons finely chopped fresh parsley
Juice of ½ lemon

Heat half the butter in a large soup pot or Dutch oven until it foams. Add the onions and garlic and sauté over low heat until the onions just begin to turn golden. Add the turnips or parsnips, celery, tomatoes and liquid, and about two-thirds of the carrots, reserving the rest for later. Pour in the water, which will not quite cover the vegetables. Bring to a boil, add the basil, thyme, and cloves, then cover and simmer over low heat until the vegetables are tender but not mushy.

With a slotted spoon, transfer the cooked vegetables, along with a bit of the cooking liquid, to the container of a food processor or blender. Process in batches to a th consistency and return the puree to the soup pot.

Heat the remaining butter in a small skillet until it foams. Sauté the reserved carrots over moderately low heat until they are golden. Stir them into the soup along with enough milk to achieve the desired consistency. Season to taste with salt and pepper. Return to low heat for 10 to 15 minutes, but don't let the soup boil. Stir in the parsley and lemon juice and serve. This soup is nice with some fresh warm bread or topped with crisp croutons.

Serves 6 to 8

Seasonings for soups may be varied to suit tastes. The simplest may have only pepper and salt, while the richest may have a little of every savor, so delicately blended that no one is conspicuous. The best seasoning is that which is made up of the smallest quantity from each of many spices. No measure can be given, because the good soup-maker must be a skillful taster.

—*The Buckeye Cookbook,* 1883

POTAGE CRESSONIER

This simple but elegant Creole soup is a good one to make a day ahead, since its flavor develops quite nicely. Serve it either hot or cold.

2½ tablespoons butter
2 medium onions, chopped
6 cups diced potatoes (scrub and leave the peel on if it looks good)
2 cups water or vegetable stock
2 large bunches watercress (about 4 to 5 packed cups)
2 cups whole or low-fat milk
Salt and freshly ground black pepper

In a large soup pot or Dutch oven, heat the butter until it foams. Add the onions and garlic and sauté over low heat until the onions are translucent. Add the potatoes and water or stock. Turn the heat up to bring to a boil, then lower the heat, cover, and simmer until the potatoes are just tender, about 15 minutes. Add the watercress and simmer for another 10 minutes. Remove from the heat.

Transfer approximately two-thirds of the solid mixture to the container of a food processor or blender with about ½ cup of the liquid. Process until smoothly pureed and stir the mixture back into the soup pot. Add the milk and season to taste with salt and pepper. Return to low heat just until thoroughly heated through. Adjust the consistency with more milk if necessary.

Serves 6

SWEET POTATO SOUP

A warming soup with an appealing golden color, it was likely developed to take advantage of the bumper crop of sweet potatoes so common to the South. Their natural sweetness is what gives this soup its surprising flavor element.

2 tablespoons butter
2 medium onions, chopped
2 medium carrots, diced
1 large stalk celery, diced
A handful of celery leaves
5 heaping cups diced (½-inch) raw sweet potato
2 bay leaves
¼ teaspoon dried thyme
¼ teaspoon ground nutmeg
1 cup whole or low-fat milk, or as needed
Salt and freshly ground black pepper

Heat the butter in a large soup pot or Dutch oven until it foams. Add the onions, carrots, and celery and sauté over low heat until the onions begin to turn golden. Add the celery leaves, sweet potato dice, bay leaves, and enough water to cover all but about 1 inch of the vegetables. Bring to a boil, add the thyme and nutmeg, then cover and simmer over low heat for about 15 minutes, or until the sweet potatoes and vegetables are tender.

With a slotted spoon, remove about half of the solid ingredients and transfer them to the container of a food processor or blender along with ½ cup of the liquid. Process until smoothly pureed, then stir back into the soup pot. Add the milk, more or less to achieve the desired consistency. Season to taste with salt and pepper. Simmer over very low heat for another 10 minutes. Serve with croutons if you'd like.

Serves 6

PARSNIP CHOWDER

Although the word *chowder* originates from the French *chaudière*, meaning "kettle," chowders have come to represent a variety of all-American soups. Most chowders are associated with New England, as is this recipe, and are usually characterized by a milk base with the addition of potatoes and other vegetables or seafood. Parsnips are hardy winter roots, and their mild flavor is just right for this soothing cold-weather soup.

2 tablespoons butter
1 cup chopped onion
4 medium potatoes, peeled and finely diced
1 pound parsnips, peeled and finely diced
3 cups water
2 cups whole or low-fat milk
3 tablespoons finely chopped fresh parsley
1 to 2 tablespoons finely chopped fresh dill, to taste
Salt and freshly ground black pepper

Many cooks do not appear to be alive to the fact that the less pretentious they make a soup the more certain it is to give satisfaction, and of all cooking, nothing is easier to do well, and nothing more difficult to do badly, than soup-making—too much pains being productive of the same results as too many cooks.

—*Godey's Lady's Book,* 1870

In a large soup pot or Dutch oven, heat the butter until it foams. Add the onions and sauté them over low heat until they are golden. Add the potatoes, parsnips, and water. Turn the heat up to bring to a boil, then lower the heat, cover, and simmer until the potatoes and parsnips are tender, about 25 minutes.

With a slotted spoon, remove 2 cups worth of the potatoes and parsnips. Mash them well and stir them back into the soup. Add the milk, parsley, and dill. Season to taste with salt and pepper. Simmer over low heat for 10 minutes, or just until thoroughly heated through.

The soup may be served at once, but if possible, let it stand for an hour or so before serving, then heat through as needed.

Serves 6

CREAM OF ASPARAGUS SOUP

Asparagus has been a much-loved kitchen-garden vegetable since colonial times, when in 1737 William Byrd wrote that he had found growing "very large and long asparagus of splendid flavor." Asparagus soups appeared with regularity in early cookbooks, often rubbed through a sieve to produce a puree.

2 pounds asparagus
2 tablespoons butter
1 large onion, chopped
1 clove garlic, minced
1 large potato, finely diced
2½ cups water or vegetable stock
1 teaspoon dried dill
½ teaspoon dried basil
Dash of nutmeg
½ to 1 cup whole or low-fat milk
Salt and freshly ground black pepper

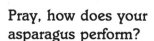

Pray, how does your asparagus perform?

—John Adams (1735–1826), in a letter to his wife, Abigail

Cut about 1 inch off the bottoms of the asparagus stalks and discard. Scrape any that appear to have tough skins with a vegetable peeler. Cut the stalks into approximately 1-inch pieces, setting aside the tips for later use.

Heat the butter in a large soup pot or Dutch oven. Add the onion and sauté until it is golden. Add the asparagus pieces, garlic, potato, water or stock, dill, basil, and nutmeg. Bring to a boil, then cover and simmer until the asparagus and potatoes are tender, about 15 minutes. Remove from the heat.

With a slotted spoon, transfer the solid ingredients to the container of a food processor or blender. Process, in batches, until smoothly pureed, then stir back into the liquid in the soup pot. Add enough milk to achieve the desired consistency; season to taste with salt and pepper. Return to low heat.

Steam the reserved asparagus tips until they are tender-crisp. Stir them into the soup and simmer over very low heat for another 5 minutes. You can either serve this at once or let it stand for an hour or so to flavor, then heat through as needed.

Serves 6

OKRA-RICE SOUP

A true southern classic, this soup was as commonplace in the nineteenth century as it is unusual today. Despite the "throw everything into the pot and simmer" simplicity of the recipe, the result is a wonderfully complex blend of flavors and textures—thanks mainly to the unique character of okra. This thick soup is closely related to a Creole gumbo and tastes great served with hot Buttermilk Biscuits (page 18).

2 tablespoons butter
2 medium onions, chopped
2 medium stalks celery, finely diced
5 cups water
6 medium ripe, juicy tomatoes, chopped
4 cups sliced (½ inch thick) young okra
1 medium green bell pepper, chopped
⅔ cup raw brown rice
3 tablespoons chopped fresh parsley
2 bay leaves
1 teaspoon dried thyme
¼ teaspoon dried red pepper flakes or ⅛ teaspoon cayenne pepper
Salt and freshly ground black pepper

In a large, porcelain-lined soup pot or Dutch oven (this is recommended so that the okra doesn't discolor), heat the butter until it foams. Add the onions and celery and sauté over low heat until the onions are just beginning to turn golden. Add the water, followed by all the remaining ingredients (be aware that even the small amount of red pepper or cayenne given here will produce a distinct hot spiciness, so use your discretion). Bring to a boil, then simmer over low heat, covered, for about 1 hour, stirring occasionally, until the rice is cooked and the vegetables are tender. Serve at once, or let the soup stand for an hour or so.

This soup will thicken considerably as it stands. Adjust the consistency if necessary with a bit more water and correct the seasonings, but let it remain very thick.

Serves 6 to 8

Hot soup at table is very vulgar; it either leads to an unseemly mode of taking it, or keeps people waiting too long whilst it cools. Soup should be brought to table only moderately warm.

—Charles Day
Hints on Etiquette, 1843

TOMATO-BARLEY SOUP

Barley soups seem to have been very common in the nineteenth century—I noticed them on a number of old restaurant menus as well as cookbooks of that period—although there didn't seem to be just one standard recipe. This particular one was inspired by a recipe from *The Virginia Housewife* (1824) by Mary Randolph, and makes for a hearty, full-flavored soup whose ingredients are readily available in the winter.

2 tablespoons safflower oil
2 large onions, quartered and thinly
    sliced
¾ cup pearl barley, rinsed
2 medium carrots, sliced
2 medium turnips or 2 smallish
    potatoes, peeled and diced
2 large stalks celery, diced
One 28-ounce can imported plum
    tomatoes with liquid, chopped
2 bay leaves
5 cups water
3 tablespoons chopped fresh dill
Salt and freshly ground black pepper

Never allow butter, soup or other food to remain in your whiskers. Use the napkin frequently.

—*Hill's Manual of Social and Business Forms*, 1879

Heat the oil in a large soup pot or Dutch oven. Add the onions and sauté over low heat until they are golden. Add the barley, carrots, turnips or potatoes, celery, tomatoes with their liquid, bay leaves, and water. Turn up the heat to bring to a boil, then lower the heat, cover, and simmer for 1¼ hours, stirring every 20 minutes or so. At this point the barley and vegetables should be done, or nearly so.

Add the dill and season to taste with salt and pepper. Simmer, covered, another 10 to 15 minutes, or until the barley is puffy and the vegetables are tender but not mushy. Adjust the consistency with more water if necessary. The soup will thicken as it stands. Adjust the liquid and seasonings as needed, but let it stay nice and thick.

Serves 8

VIRGINIA PEANUT SOUP

The peanut was originally cultivated by the Indians of South America, very possibly of Brazil, and enjoyed a remarkably long trip to many parts of the world before it returned to our colonial shores. Bearing its African name of *goober*, the peanut came back to us aboard slave ships. Not until George Washington Carver promoted it in the latter part of the nineteenth century, however, did it become an important crop. Carver, the noted botanist and inventor, developed numerous recipes for the peanut, which he believed to be an important and nutritious food. Some attribute this famous southern soup to him, at least in its refined version. Admittedly rich, this soup has an intense and unusual flavor and is good either hot or cold. Here is my interpretation.

2 tablespoons butter
4 cups water or vegetable stock
1 cup chopped onion
2 large stalks celery, finely diced
3 medium carrots, thinly sliced
2½ tablespoons unbleached white
  flour
3 tablespoons dry red wine or
  sherry
A few grains of cayenne pepper
⅔ cup peanut butter
1½ cups whole or low-fat milk
Salt and freshly ground black pepper
Chopped roasted peanuts for garnish
Minced fresh parsley for garnish

In a large soup pot or Dutch oven, heat the butter with 3 tablespoons of the water or stock until the butter melts. Add the onions, celery, and carrots and cook over low heat, stirring frequently, until the onions begin to turn golden. Sprinkle in the flour and continue to cook, stirring constantly, until the mixture begins to turn golden brown.

Add the remaining water or stock, the wine or sherry, and the cayenne. Bring to a boil, then cover and simmer over low heat until the vegetables are tender, about 10 to 15 minutes. Spoon the peanut butter into the pot and whisk it in briskly until blended with the stock. Stir in the milk and season to taste with salt and pepper (season slowly and carefully and taste as you do—you don't want to overpower the unusual peanut flavor with too much salt and pepper). Bring to a simmer and cook over very low heat for another 10 minutes or so, stirring occasionally. If time allows, let the soup stand for an hour or so to thicken before serving, then heat through as needed. Garnish each serving with some chopped peanuts and parsley.

Serves 6

At the turn of the century, the word *peanut* was used to describe petty or mean-spirited politics. The *New York Evening Post* in 1909 put it this way: "They used to talk about 'peanut politics' at Albany, but a peanut is too large and respectable an object to yield comparison for yesterday's action of the Senate."

ZUCCHINI CHOWDER

This excellent southwestern soup recipe was given to me by a friend who grew up in San Antonio, Texas. He remembers having had it at home and said that it was quite typical in the area. Serve it with Zuni Quick Bread (page 35) or Buttermilk-Corn Bread (page 28).

2 tablespoons safflower oil
1 heaping cup chopped onion
2 cloves garlic, minced
1 large green bell pepper, diced
1 cup chopped ripe tomato
7 to 8 cups diced zucchini
½ teaspoon each dried oregano,
    ground cumin, and chile powder
1½ cups whole or low-fat milk
½ cup grated Monterey Jack cheese
2 tablespoons minced fresh cilantro
    or parsley
Salt and freshly ground black pepper

Heat the oil in a small skillet. Add the onions and garlic and sauté over low heat until the onions are translucent. Add the green pepper and continue to sauté until it is tender-crisp. Add the chopped tomatoes and sauté for another two minutes or so, just until they have softened somewhat.

Place the zucchini dice in a large soup pot or Dutch oven with about 1 inch of water. Cover and steam over moderately low heat until the zucchini dice are just tender, lifting the lid frequently to stir so that they will cook evenly. Remove 1½ cups of the zucchini dice and set aside.

Stir the skillet mixture into the remaining zucchini in the soup pot. Transfer the mixture, in batches, to the container of a food processor or blender and process until smoothly pureed. Return the puree to the pot along with the reserved zucchini dice, seasonings, and enough milk to achieve the desired consistency. Return to low heat and sprinkle in the grated cheese and the cilantro or parsley. Season to taste with salt and pepper. Simmer over very low heat for 10 to 15 minutes, making sure that the soup does not boil.

Serves 6

Many people make a disgusting noise with their lips, by inhaling their breath strongly whilst taking soup—a habit which should be carefully avoided.

—Charles Day
Hints on Etiquette, 1843

Wrong way to finish soup: Slurping from tipped bowl is unseemly & noisy.

POTATO, CHEESE, AND GREEN CHILE SOUP

I discovered this robust soup in a number of Tex-Mex cafes and was glad to learn that it is a southwestern standard.

4 medium potatoes, peeled and
  diced
5 cups water or vegetable stock
2 tablespoons safflower or olive oil
1 large onion, chopped
2 to 3 cloves garlic, crushed or
  minced
1 large green bell pepper, finely
  chopped
1 heaping cup finely chopped ripe
  tomatoes (substitute canned
  imported tomatoes if necessary)
1 cup cooked fresh corn kernels
  (substitute frozen if necessary)
One 4-ounce can mild green chiles,
  drained and chopped
½ teaspoon ground cumin
½ teaspoon dried oregano
½ pound Monterey Jack cheese,
  grated
Salt and freshly ground black pepper

Place the potato dice in a large soup pot or Dutch oven and cover with the water or vegetable stock. Bring to a boil, then cover and simmer over low heat until the potatoes are just tender, about 15 minutes.

In the meantime, heat the oil in a small skillet. Sauté the onions over low heat until they are translucent. Add the garlic and green pepper and sauté until the mixture begins to brown lightly.

Remove half the potatoes from their cooking liquid with a slotted spoon and mash well. Stir the mashed potatoes back into the soup pot along with the skillet mixture, tomatoes, corn, green chiles, cumin, and oregano. Simmer over low heat for 20 minutes.

Sprinkle in the grated cheese, just a small amount at a time, stirring it in until it "disappears" each time. Season to taste with salt and pepper and allow the soup to simmer over very low heat, stirring frequently, for another 5 minutes. You can either serve this soup at once or let it stand an hour or so before serving. Heat through as needed.

Serves 6

Correct way to finish soup: Licking the bowl is both quiet & dignified.

COLD AVOCADO SOUP

This quick and easy southwestern soup is a natural choice to refresh you on a hot summer day.

2 large, ripe avocados
2½ cups low-fat milk
1 small green bell pepper, finely
    chopped
2 bunches scallions, minced
2 tablespoons finely chopped
    cilantro or fresh parsley
Juice of ½ lemon
½ teaspoon ground cumin
Salt and freshly ground black pepper
4 corn tortillas for garnish

Peel the avocados. Mash one of them well and finely dice the other one. Place the mashed avocado in a serving vessel and add ½ cup of the milk. Stir them together until smooth, then add all the remaining ingredients except the tortillas and stir again until well blended. Cover and chill the soup until you are ready to serve it.

Just before serving, cut the tortillas into approximately ½-by-2-inch strips. Toast them in a hot, dry heavy skillet until they are crisp, stirring frequently. Serve the chilled soup garnished with the crisp tortilla strips.

Serves 4 to 6

PUREE OF GARBANZO SOUP

This flavorful, traditional soup of the Southwest requires very little effort, but needs several hours' cooking time.

2½ cups raw garbanzos (chick-peas)
2 tablespoons safflower oil
1 heaping cup chopped onion
2 to 3 cloves garlic
One 14-ounce can imported
    tomatoes with liquid, chopped
1 teaspoon dried oregano
1 teaspoon ground cumin, or to
    taste
½ teaspoon ground coriander
Salt and freshly ground black pepper
1 cup grated Cheddar cheese
    (optional)
Chopped cilantro or fresh parsley for
    garnish

Sort and rinse the beans and soak them overnight in plenty of water.

When you're ready to cook them, drain and rinse them again and place them in a large soup pot or Dutch oven with water in 1½ times their bulk. Stir in the oil and simmer until they are just tender, about 2 hours. Add all the remaining ingredients and simmer for another hour, or until the garbanzos are quite tender and the onions are cooked. Transfer the solid ingredients to the container of a food processor or blender, reserving about 1½ cups. Add a bit of the cooking liquid and process until smoothly pureed. Stir the puree back into the soup pot along with the reserved garbanzos. Return to very low heat for just a few minutes. If you choose to add the cheese, sprinkle it in, a bit at a time, stirring until it melts. Garnish each serving with some chopped cilantro or parsley.

Serves 6

SQUASH AND CORN CHOWDER

This recipe is adapted from one that comes by way of the American Indians of the upper Mississippi River area. The perfect time to make it is in the late summer and early autumn, when the first of the squash harvest overlaps with the tail end of the fresh sweet corn crop.

1 medium butternut squash (about
   1½ pounds)
1 heaping cup chopped onion
2 medium potatoes, scrubbed and
   diced
Water or vegetable stock
2 tablespoons butter
2 bay leaves
½ teaspoon dried thyme
½ teaspoon dried summer savory
2½ to 3 cups cooked fresh corn
   kernels (about 3 medium ears,
   scraped)
1 cup whole or low-fat milk
Salt and freshly ground black pepper

With a sharp knife, cut the squash across the center of the rounded part. Remove the seeds and stringy fibers. Slice the squash into ½ inch rings, then pare each ring and chop into small dice.

Place the squash dice in a large soup pot or Dutch oven along with the chopped onions and potatoes and add enough water or vegetable stock to cover all but about 1 inch of the vegetables, leaving them above the water level. Bring to a boil, then add the butter, bay leaves, thyme, and savory. Cover and simmer over low heat, stirring once or twice, until the squash and potatoes are tender, about 20 to 25 minutes.

With a slotted spoon, scoop out 2 heaping cups of the solid ingredients, mash them well, and stir them back into the soup. Add the cooked fresh corn kernels and more or less of the milk as needed to achieve the desired consistency. Season to taste with salt and freshly ground pepper and simmer over very low heat for another 10 to 15 minutes. You may serve this at once, but if time allows, let the soup stand an hour or so before serving, then heat through as needed. This may also be done a day ahead, since it flavors nicely overnight.

Serves 6 to 8

**We dined on Indian corn
and Squash soop, and
boiled bread.**

—John Bartram
   Observations in his Travels,
   1751

CAJUN CORN SOUP

This beautiful, creamy soup is perfect for taking advantage of summer's bumper crop of sweet corn. Serve it either hot or cold.

6 medium ears fresh corn
1½ tablespoons safflower oil
1½ cups chopped onions
3 cloves garlic, minced
3 cups water
¼ teaspoon dried red pepper flakes,
    or to taste
¼ teaspoon dried thyme
1 tablespoon butter
1 large green or red bell pepper,
    finely diced
1 cup whole or low-fat milk
Salt to taste

Before starting the soup, scrape the corn kernels off the cob with a sharp knife. Set aside.

Heat the oil in a large soup pot or Dutch oven. Add the onions and garlic and sauté over low heat until the onions are lightly golden. Add the corn kernels, water, red pepper flakes (this amount will produce a very nippy hotness, so adjust it to your taste), and thyme. Bring to a boil, then cover and simmer over low heat until the corn kernels are tender but not overdone. The time this takes will vary greatly according to the type and age of the corn, so check frequently. Remove from the heat.

With a slotted spoon, transfer half the solid ingredients to the container of a food processor or blender along with a small amount of the liquid. Process until smoothly pureed and stir back into the soup pot.

Heat the butter in a small skillet until it foams. Add the green or red pepper and sauté until it is touched with brown. Stir it into the soup, followed by the milk. Season to taste with salt. Return to low heat for 5 minutes. Serve at once or chill.

Serves 6

It is best to plant corn once the Baltimore orioles appear.

—American folk belief

DUTCH CORN AND CABBAGE SOUP

Several of the standard Pennsylvania Dutch ingredients are combined in a very pleasant soup. Serve it with Potato Dumplings, whose recipe is given below.

2 tablespoons butter
1 large onion, chopped
2 tablespoons unbleached white flour
4 cups finely shredded cabbage
1 large potato, finely diced
3 cups raw corn kernels (3 to 4 ears)
1 heaping cup chopped ripe
    tomatoes or the equivalent of
    drained canned tomatoes
4½ cups water or vegetable stock
1½ teaspoons mixed dried herbs of
    your choice
½ cup whole or low-fat milk
Salt and freshly ground black pepper
Minced fresh parsley for garnish

In a large soup pot or Dutch oven, heat the butter until it foams. Add the onion and sauté until it is golden. Sprinkle in the flour and stir it in until blended. Add the cabbage, potato, corn, tomatoes, and water or stock. Bring to a boil, sprinkle in the herbs, and simmer, covered, over low heat until all the vegetables are tender, about 30 minutes. Stir in the milk, more or less as needed to achieve the desired consistency. Season to taste with salt and pepper and simmer for another 10 minutes over very low heat. Do not boil. Allow the soup to stand for an hour or more before serving to develop flavor. Heat through as needed before serving. Garnish each serving with a bit of minced parsley.

Serves 6

POTATO DUMPLINGS

These Pennsylvania Dutch dumplings are easy to make and add to soups an extra measure of the filling goodness that Dutch cooking is known for.

1 cup smoothly mashed potato
1 egg, beaten
½ cup whole wheat flour
½ cup unbleached white flour
½ teaspoon salt
½ teaspoon baking powder
Dash of nutmeg

Combine the mashed potato with the beaten egg. Stir the flours together along with the salt, baking powder, and nutmeg. Work this into the mashed-potato mixture, bit by bit, to form a soft dough. If time allows, chill the dough, which will make it easier to work with.

With floured hands (the dough will be slightly sticky), shape the dough into 1-inch-round balls. Bring a deep, heavy saucepan full of water to a rolling boil. Drop the dumplings gently into the water, one by one, only half at a time if necessary so that they are not on top of one another. They will drop to the bottom at first; after a minute or so, gently nudge them with a wooden spoon so that they don't stick. Cook at a gentle boil for 10 minutes. Remove with a slotted spoon.

Makes 15 to 18 dumplings

Chapter 4
SALADS

If a gentleman with whom you are acquainted has dressed a salad, and offers the plate to you, take what you want, and immediately return to him the remainder; and do not pass it on to persons in your vicinity. It is *his* privilege and not *yours* to offer it to others, as he has had the trouble of dressing it.

—Eliza Leslie
The Behavior Book, 1853

Finding interesting regional salads to include in this chapter was not as simple as I'd imagined it would be. In old cookbooks, the salad chapter would often seem to be there because it was obligatory, and in my travels, I was often disappointed not to find a single salad with regional interest on any given menu. I don't believe, though, that this is because yesterday's cooks were unimaginative salad makers. To the contrary, I'm inclined to think that since making a salad is such an improvisational business, relying on what's available and using a little of this and that, salad recipes just weren't as standardized as, say, a recipe for corn muffins. Therefore there was little need for setting them down in writing.

Several of the nineteenth-century cookbooks I read spent more time giving advice on how to dress a salad than on how to make the salad itself. If you think about it, this is perfectly reasonable. Given that if one had just gone out to the kitchen-garden to pick some fresh chervil, watercress, savoy cabbage, or any of the other mouthwatering greens that were well loved in those days, there was little need for obsessive instructions on what or how much to use—just dress and season and eat!

Old cookbooks were full of stern or frivolous advice, too. Maria Parloa, in her *Kitchen Companion* (1887), warns, "A vegetable salad may be a thing of beauty or an indistinct mixture and uninviting dish." A depression-era cookbook from Wichita urges us to arrange a salad "daintily."

After an arduous search, I ended up with what I think is a selection of offbeat and pleasing salads. Most use vegetables usually reserved for cooking, as well as beans and grains in colorful, well-seasoned ways. The list of ingredients reads like a "who's who" (or should I say "what's what") of American staples: Cabbage, potatoes, corn, peas, pinto beans, rice, avocados, and even Jerusalem artichokes and tortillas. You'll find regional variations of what must be the number-one great American salad, cole slaw, as well as more exotic selections from most every locale around the country.

CABBAGE AND PEPPER SLAW

Cole slaws (from the Dutch, *kool*, for "cabbage," and *sla*, for "salad"), to my mind, are the true all-American salads, being part of almost every regional repertoire across the country. The numerous varieties made it tough to choose which ones to include. One of those that I especially enjoy is this recipe, one of many southern variations, in which the slaw is dressed in oil and vinegar, so that as it stands, it becomes more and more like a pickle.

5 cups firmly packed shredded
   cabbage
1 large green or red bell pepper, cut
   into thin julienne strips
1 large stalk celery, finely chopped
1 small onion, minced
2 tablespoons capers (optional)

Dressing:
¼ cup safflower oil
¼ cup cider vinegar
½ teaspoon salt
½ teaspoon granulated sugar
½ teaspoon celery seed or dill seed
Freshly ground black pepper to taste

They prefer cabbages to roses.

—George W. Curtis
The Potiphar Papers, 1853

The cabbage should not be too finely shredded (a food processor will make it too fine). Combine it with next 4 ingredients in a serving bowl. Combine the dressing ingredients in a small bowl and let them stand until the salt and sugar dissolve. Mix well and toss together with the cabbage mixture. Refrigerate for at least two hours before serving, stirring occasionally to distribute the dressing.

Serves 4 to 6

NORTH CAROLINA RELISH SLAW

A friend who grew up in the western part of North Carolina contributed this recipe, commenting that the addition of relish makes it a favorite to serve with fish. Whether you eat fish or not, you'll find that the relish adds a very unusual touch.

2 cups packed finely shredded white
   cabbage
2 cups packed finely shredded red
   cabbage
1 large carrot, grated
⅓ cup pickle relish
2 bunches scallions, minced
½ cup mayonnaise (see below)
2 teaspoons prepared mustard
1 to 2 tablespoons lemon juice
Salt and freshly ground black pepper

Combine all the ingredients in a serving bowl, seasoning to taste with the lemon juice, salt, and pepper. Toss well until thoroughly mixed. That's it!

Serves 4 to 6

The table was soon spread and garnished, from pepper-castor to cold-slaw.

—*Knickerbocker Magazine,* 1842

HOMEMADE MAYONNAISE

I rarely use mayonnaise anymore, preferring lighter dressings for most salads. However, on those occasions that call for it, I like making a fresh batch, since it's so quick and easy to make in a food processor. The safflower oil makes this a dressing that's low in saturated fat.

1 small egg
1½ tablespoons lemon juice
½ teaspoon prepared mustard
¼ teaspoon salt
1 cup safflower oil

In the container of a food processor, combine the first 4 ingredients. Process for several seconds, until smooth and light. With the food processor on, add the oil, ¼ cup at a time, through the feed tube. Once all the oil is in, continue to process for only a few more seconds.

Makes about 1 cup

CREAMY COLE SLAW

This mild and pleasant slaw is based on the New England variant. It complements the flavor of sweet-and-sour dishes, such as Baked Barbecue Beans (page 105), quite nicely.

4 cups firmly packed finely
   shredded cabbage
1 medium carrot, finely grated
¼ cup chopped fresh herbs of your
   choice (a combination of parsley
   and dill is nice)

Dressing:
¾ cup sour cream or a mixture of
   half sour cream and half yogurt
1 tablespoon cider vinegar
1 tablespoon safflower oil
½ teaspoon salt
½ teaspoon dry mustard
¼ teaspoon paprika
Freshly ground black pepper to taste

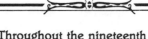

Throughout the nineteenth and early twentieth centuries, the principal ingredient of cole-slaw went through a variety of meanings as a slang expression. In the nineteenth century, *cabbage* was a term describing money or banknotes and was even used as a verb meaning "to obtain dishonestly." In the 1940s, it was a slang word for a young girl; Billy Rose, in a 1947 newspaper column said, "The little cabbage spoke up for her generation."

In a serving bowl, combine the cabbage, carrot, and herbs. In a small mixing bowl, combine all the dressing ingredients and stir together until well blended. Pour over the cabbage mixture and toss together until thoroughly mixed. This may be served at once or refrigerated an hour or so until needed.

Serves 4 to 6

JERUSALEM ARTICHOKE SALAD

Jerusalem artichokes are bumpy tubers that are not artichokes, nor do they have anything to do with Jerusalem. They are the root of a native American sunflower, first noted in 1605 as a garden crop of Cape Cod Indians. A truly unique vegetable, they may be used raw or cooked and are highly nutritious. Their flavor and texture are somewhat of a cross between potatoes, turnips, and water chestnuts. They are occasionally marketed under the name "sunchokes" and are available in late summer and early fall. Needless to say, they make for a very unusual, crunchy salad.

1 pound Jerusalem artichokes
2 bunches scallions, finely chopped
2 tablespoons fresh mint leaves,
    minced, or 2 teaspoons dried
    mint
2 or 3 tablespoons minced fresh dill
¼ cup (scant) safflower oil
¼ cup (scant) cider vinegar
1 tablespoon honey
3 tablespoons sunflower seeds,
    toasted
2 cups chopped dark-green lettuce
    leaves

Scrub the Jerusalem artichokes well. Trim off any excessively dark or knobby spots, but you don't have to peel them. Cut them into thin, bite-sized pieces and place them in a serving bowl along with the scallions, mint, and dill.

In a small bowl, combine the oil, vinegar, and honey and stir together until well blended. Pour this over the artichoke mixture, toss well, and allow to stand, covered and refrigerated, for 1 hour. Give the mixture one good stir during this time.

Before serving, add the sunflower seeds and lettuce and toss well again. If you're short on time, you may skip the 1 hour of refrigeration. The salad will taste nearly as good.

Serves 4 to 6

CORN RELISH SALAD

Derived from the Pennsylvania Dutch tradition, this recipe is closely related to one of the famous "seven sweets and seven sours," as their relishes are known. In salad form, I have seen it referred to also as Amish Corn Salad. Simple to make, it is as colorful as it is tasty.

4 cups cooked fresh corn kernels
   (about 5 ears)
1 medium green bell pepper, cut
   into 1-inch strips
1 small red bell pepper, cut as
   above
1 cup finely shredded cabbage
1 small onion, halved and thinly
   sliced

Dressing:
¼ cup safflower oil
¼ cup cider vinegar
2 teaspoons honey
½ teaspoon dry mustard
½ teaspoon celery seed or dill seed
Salt and freshly ground black pepper

Combine all the salad ingredients in a serving bowl. In a small bowl, combine all the dressing ingredients and stir until well blended. Pour the dressing over the corn mixture and toss well. Cover and allow to marinate, refrigerated, for several hours. Stir occasionally to distribute the marinade.

Serves 6 to 8

And out in Iowa, where the black loam is twenty feet deep, the corn grows so high they have to climb ladders to get down the ears.

—Max Adeler (1847–1915)
Ten Tall Tales

POTATO SALAD (With Boiled Dressing)

Perhaps after cole slaw, potato salads must run a close second as a much-loved American salad with many regional variations. This recipe is a New England type, and what makes it special—and very nice—is the traditional boiled dressing.

6 medium potatoes
1 large stalk celery, finely diced
1 medium green bell pepper, finely
   chopped
¼ cup chopped green olives or pickles
2 bunches scallions, finely chopped
2 to 3 tablespoons chopped fresh
   parsley or dill, or a little of both
2 hard-boiled eggs, chopped (optional)
1 recipe Old-Fashioned Boiled
   Dressing (recipe follows)
Salt and freshly ground black pepper

Cook the potatoes in their skins until tender but still firm. Let cool, then peel and dice them. In a large bowl, combine the potatoes with all the remaining ingredients and season to taste with salt and pepper. Toss well to combine. This salad may be served either chilled or at room temperature.

Serves 6 to 8

OLD-FASHIONED BOILED DRESSING

A traditional dressing used in old New England, midwestern, and occasionally southern home cooking, boiled dressing was commonly used in slaws and "cooked" salads, such as potato salads. It was most often made with an egg yolk or two, but I have left that out, finding that the dressing is thick and flavorful enough without it.

1 tablespoon butter
2 tablespoons unbleached white flour
1 cup whole or low-fat milk
1 teaspoon dry mustard
A few grains of cayenne pepper
¼ cup cider vinegar

Heat the butter in a saucepan until it melts. Sprinkle in the flour, stirring carefully until it is smoothly blended with the butter. Add the milk, ¼ cup at a time, stirring briskly to avoid lumping. Stir in the dry mustard and cayenne and let the sauce bubble gently until it is thick, about 8 to 10 minutes. Slowly stir in the vinegar and bring to a gentle boil. Let the dressing cool before using it on a salad.

Makes about one cup

GREEN PEA AND CHEDDAR CHEESE SALAD

Here is a salad that pleases both the eye and the palate. I enjoyed it several times while traveling in the Midwest—particularly Kansas, Oklahoma, and Iowa. Not having found it in any old midwestern cookbooks, I concluded that it must be a relatively recent invention. Its constant ingredients seem to be the peas, cheese, and celery, with additional items, which vary. This is my version, a composite of all those that I sampled.

2 cups fresh shelled green peas, steamed
1 cup mushrooms, sliced and steamed
1 cup firmly packed grated Cheddar cheese
1 large stalk celery, finely diced
1 small red bell pepper, finely diced
5 or 6 radishes, halved and sliced
1 to 2 tablespoons minced fresh dill
3 tablespoons safflower oil
2 tablespoons cider vinegar
Salt and freshly ground black pepper

Combine all the ingredients except the salt and pepper in a serving bowl and toss well. Season lightly with salt and pepper and toss again. Serve at once.

Serves 4 to 6

You are welcome, dear, welcome as green peas in June, or radishes in March.

—Ann S. Stephens
Fashion and Famine, 1854

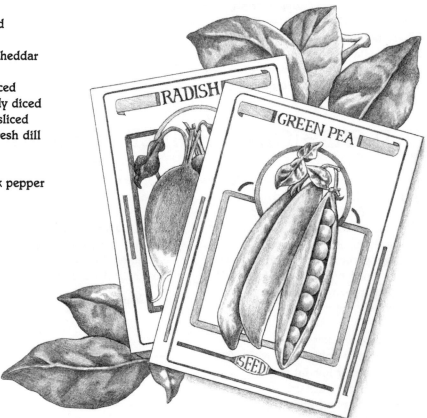

TEXAS CAVIAR (Marinated Black-eyed Pea Salad)

The black-eyed pea has been one of the most important staples of Southern cookery since it was brought to the South from Africa as part of the slave trade. This appetizing salad is known from traditional Texas home cooking, and its name certainly implies the high esteem in which black-eye peas are held.

3 cups cooked black-eyed peas
1 large green bell pepper, cut into 1-inch-thin julienne strips
2 to 3 bunches scallions, chopped
⅓ cup chopped fresh parsley
¼ cup mixed equal parts olive oil and safflower oil
¼ cup cider vinegar
½ teaspoon dried oregano
½ teaspoon dried basil
Salt and freshly ground black pepper
Dark-green lettuce leaves
2 hard-boiled eggs, chopped (optional)

In a serving bowl, combine all the ingredients except the lettuce leaves and chopped eggs and toss well. Allow the salad to marinate, refrigerated, for several hours.

Arrange each serving atop a bed of lettuce leaves, garnished with a bit of the optional chopped egg.

Serves 6

Her menu, in which corn-bread, dried fruit and blackeyed pease . . . figured as the principal dishes.

—T. N. Page
Red Rock, 1898

MENU

Corn-bread;
Dried fruit, all sorts;
Black-eyed pease,
in great abundance.

SUMMER SQUASH AND STRING BEAN SALAD

This appealing mix of steamed vegetables and garbanzos is adapted from *Early California Hospitality* (1938), a collection of early Mission recipes of the Southwest.

2 small yellow summer squashes
2 cups string beans, cut into 1-inch
  pieces
1 cup cooked garbanzos (chick-peas)
1 small onion, minced
2 tablespoons chopped fresh parsley
¼ cup (scant) equal parts mixed
  olive oil and safflower oil
¼ cup (scant) cider vinegar
Salt and freshly ground black pepper
½ teaspoon dried oregano
Dark-green lettuce leaves

Scrub the squashes, cut them in half lengthwise, and slice them about ¼ inch thick. Steam them until they are tender-crisp. At the same time, steam the cut string beans separately until they, too, are tender-crisp. Once they are done, refresh the vegetables immediately under cold water. Let them drain for a few minutes in a colander.

Combine the squash and string beans in a large serving bowl along with all the remaining ingredients except the lettuce. Toss well and refrigerate for several hours, covered, stirring every so often to distribute the marinade. Place each serving atop a bed of lettuce leaves.

Serves 6

PINTO BEAN SALAD

The favored bean of the Southwest occasionally finds its way into salads.

3 cups cooked pinto beans
2 large stalks celery, finely diced
1 small green or red bell pepper,
  finely diced
2 bunches scallions, minced
3 tablespoons chopped fresh parsley
¼ cup sour cream
2 teaspoons prepared mustard
3 tablespoons safflower oil
2 tablespoons cider vinegar
1 teaspoon dried oregano
Salt and freshly ground black pepper
Dark-green lettuce leaves

Combine the first 5 ingredients in a serving bowl. In a small bowl, combine the sour cream, mustard, oil, vinegar, and oregano. Stir together until well blended, then add to the bean mixture and toss well. Add salt and pepper to taste and toss again. Serve at once, placing each serving atop a bed of lettuce leaves.

Serves 4 to 6

TACO SALAD

I first had this salad at a friend's home in Washington, D.C., and then later discovered it in restaurants in the Southwest. So named because it utilizes the standard taco ingredients, this very tasty salad is quick and easy to prepare and is a perfect choice when you'd like a hearty main-dish salad.

4 corn tortillas
2 medium firm, ripe tomatoes, chopped
1 large green bell pepper, chopped
¼ cup black olives, chopped
2 bunches scallions, minced
1 cup grated Monterey Jack or Cheddar cheese
1 cup cooked pinto or kidney beans
Dark-green lettuce, torn, as needed

Dressing:
⅓ cup thick tomato juice or tomato puree
3 tablespoons safflower oil
2 tablespoons red wine vinegar
½ teaspoon chili powder
½ teaspoon oregano
¼ teaspoon salt
Freshly ground black pepper

Over moderate heat, toast each tortilla on a dry, heavy skillet on both sides until it is crisp. Allow the tortillas to cool, then crumble into bite-sized pieces.

Combine the tortilla bits with the remaining salad ingredients in a serving bowl. The amount of lettuce you will use will vary according to the number of servings you will need.

In a small bowl, combine the dressing ingredients and stir together until well blended. Pour over the salad and toss well.

Serves 4 to 6

If possible, when combining vegetables, have those which are of a delicate flavor form the body of a salad, using only a small proportion of those with strong flavor.

—Maria Parloa
Miss Parloa's Kitchen Companion, 1887

SOUTHWESTERN RICE SALAD

The salads on these two pages are adapted from *Cuisines of the American Southwest,* by Anne Lindsay Greer, an expert on foods of that region. They're both very special salads, full of exciting flavors, textures, and colors.

1 tablespoon olive oil
2 cloves garlic, minced
1 large sweet red bell pepper, cut
    into medium julienne strips
1 large firm, ripe avocado, diced
Juice of ½ lemon
2½ cups cold cooked brown rice
1 cup cooked pinto beans
2 tablespoons minced cilantro or
    fresh parsley
½ teaspoon dried oregano
¼ cup safflower oil
2 tablespoons red wine vinegar
Salt and freshly ground black pepper

In a small skillet, heat the olive oil. Add the garlic and red bell pepper and sauté over low heat until the pepper is tender-crisp. Remove from the heat.

In a large serving bowl, combine the diced avocado with the lemon juice and toss gently. Add the skillet mixture followed by all the remaining ingredients. Season to taste with salt and pepper and toss until thoroughly mixed. Serve at once.

Serves 4 to 6

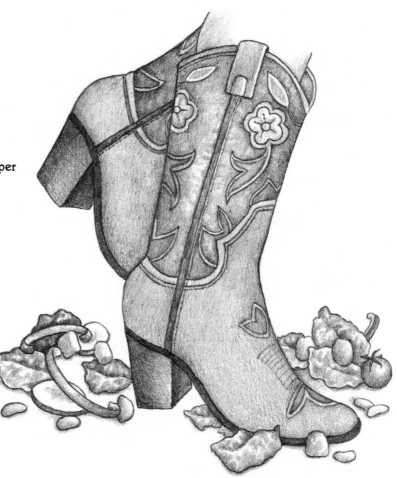

CAULIFLOWER·AND·AVOCADO SALAD

Like the recipe on the previous page, this colorful salad is adapted from Greer's *Cuisines of the American Southwest*. It makes for a very special addition to a meal with a Southwestern theme.

1 medium-small head cauliflower
1 large firm, ripe avocado, diced
Juice of ½ lemon
1 medium red bell pepper, cut into
   small julienne strips
2 bunches scallions, finely chopped

Dressing:
¼ cup mixed equal parts safflower
   oil and olive oil
3 tablespoons red wine vinegar
1 teaspoon dried oregano
½ teaspoon ground cumin
¼ teaspoon salt
Freshly ground black pepper to taste
Tomato wedges for garnish

As a Back Bay friend was saying, "You just don't find service like this anymore," one of the servitors clearing off an adjoining table let an almost complete avocado salad slip off a plate and onto the floor where it lay totally bewildered for a good ten minutes.

"There's a salad on the floor," I said to our waiter at length, which precipitated a hubbub as the herbacious material was removed.

—Richard Bissell
How Many Miles to Galena?, 1968

Break the cauliflower into bite-sized pieces and florets. Steam until tender-crisp and refresh immediately under cold water to stop the steaming. Allow the cauliflower to drain for a few minutes in a colander.

In a serving bowl, combine the diced avocado and lemon juice and toss gently. Add the cauliflower, red pepper strips, and scallions.

In a small bowl, combine the dressing ingredients and stir together until well blended. Pour over the cauliflower and avocado mixture and toss gently. Cover and refrigerate for about 1 hour before serving. Stir once or twice during that time to distribute the dressing.

Serves 4 to 6

Chapter 5
EGGS

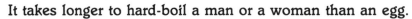

It takes longer to hard-boil a man or a woman than an egg.

—F. L. Allen
Only Yesterday, 1931

Eggs, the folkloric symbols of new life and one of nature's most perfect foods, are now, despite their innocent looks, the center of controversy. Many of us are modifying our intake of eggs until it is clearer just how cholesterol affects us. Everybody has different needs and tolerances, and moderation is always a good approach. I love eggs myself, but prefer to walk on the side of caution—since I use eggs as a cooking ingredient, I prepare them as a main dish only occasionally. The recipes here are devised so that each serving contains only one or one and a half eggs, and I've chosen a small but very select group that are truly unique and exciting.

Dominating this brief (but hopefully pithy) chapter are classic egg recipes from the Southwest, most of which I was fortunate enough to have been able to sample while traveling. Their presentation of eggs is quite exquisite and most creatively embellished with the characteristic ingredients of the region—liberally doused with the "Spanish" seasonings of tomatoes, chiles, and garlic, or intertwined in one way or another with tortillas.

Second in line with interesting egg recipes are those from the Creole tradition of New Orleans, whose gift for seasoning makes any recipe really special. In most other places, though, I found that, as an old American saying goes, "eggs is eggs," although all across the South and through Texas, a morning meal of scrambled egg with grits was something I looked forward to with great relish.

HUEVOS RANCHEROS (Ranch-Style Eggs)

Huevos Rancheros is perhaps the most widely traveled of southwestern egg dishes, having settled into brunch menus in Tex-Mex restaurants from coast to coast. There are several ways of preparing it, subject to regional variation. In New Mexico, the eggs are smothered with pure, incendiary green or red chiles; the spiced tomato-based sauce used in the following recipe is a California-style variation. Great for brunch or supper, this basic recipe for four can be easily doubled for eight.

Sauce:
1½ tablespoons safflower oil
1 medium onion, chopped
1 clove garlic, minced
1 small green or red bell pepper, diced
1 heaping cup ripe tomatoes, chopped, or 1 cup canned imported tomatoes, drained and chopped
1 cup thick tomato sauce
One 4-ounce can mild or hot green chiles, drained and chopped
1 tablespoon minced cilantro (optional)
½ teaspoon dried oregano
¼ teaspoon ground cumin
Salt to taste

Butter for frying
4 eggs
4 corn tortillas
1 cup grated Monterey Jack cheese
1 medium firm, ripe avocado, sliced, for garnish

Heat the oil in a medium skillet. Add the onion and garlic and sauté over low heat until the onion is translucent. Add the green or red pepper and continue to sauté until the onion is golden. Add the remaining sauce ingredients and simmer over low heat, covered, for 15 minutes.

Using just enough butter to cover the bottom of a small skillet, fry each egg individually to your (or your guest's) liking.

To assemble, pass each tortilla briefly through the sauce to soften (tongs are good for this), then place each on an individual plate. Top each tortilla with a fried egg, followed by some sauce and a sprinkling of grated cheese. Garnish with avocado slices. Serve at once.

Serves 4

Eggs is like autos—th' minute we pay less than th' top price we git int' cheap construction.

—Kin Hubbard
Abe Martin on Things in General, 1925

MEXICAN OMELET

I would rather that this were more correctly named New Mexican Omelet, as this recipe comes from the Apple Tree restaurant in Taos. Their cook, F. Leo Kendall, who kindly contributed this recipe, explained that it's simply a generic name for this local omelet, which features specific ingredients in various presentations.

Filling:
1 tablespoon safflower oil
2 cups chopped ripe tomatoes
3 large bunches scallions, finely chopped
2 tablespoons minced cilantro or fresh parsley
½ teaspoon dried oregano
Salt and freshly ground black pepper

6 eggs, beaten
2 tablespoons whole or low-fat milk
2 tablespoons butter
1⅓ cups grated Monterey Jack cheese
1 recipe Green Chile Sauce (page 149)
Sour cream for topping
Extra minced scallions for garnish

Heat the safflower oil in a small skillet. Add all the filling ingredients and sauté over low heat for 2 minutes or so, just until the tomato is somewhat softened. Cover and set aside.

Beat 3 of the eggs well with 1 tablespoon of the milk. Heat half of the butter in a 10-inch, nonstick Silverstone skillet. When the skillet is hot enough to make a drop of water sizzle, pour in the eggs. As they begin to set, lift the sides with a spatula and tip the skillet to allow the uncooked egg to run underneath. When the top is fairly set, arrange half of the filling on one side of the omelet, sprinkle half the cheese over it, and fold the other side over. Slide the omelet out onto a plate and cover with a matching plate to keep warm. Repeat the procedure with the remaining eggs, milk, butter, filling, and cheese.

Cut each omelet in half and arrange the portions on 4 serving plates. Spoon the Green Chile Sauce over them, followed by a small dollop of sour cream. Sprinkle each omelet with a bit of minced scallion for garnish. Serve at once.

Serves 4

EGGS WITH AVOCADO SAUCE

In several New Mexican restaurants, I encountered egg dishes enlivened with avocado pieces, either inside or atop the eggs. The combination is decidedly rich, but the blend of flavors is seductive. This is my interpretation, a composite of those that I tried, presented as a flat omelet.

2 tablespoons butter
½ medium red bell pepper, finely chopped
2 to 3 bunches scallions, minced
1 tablespoon minced mild or hot green chile (optional)
1 large firm, ripe avocado, finely diced
Juice of ½ lemon
1 tablespoon finely chopped cilantro or fresh parsley
½ cup sour cream
½ teaspoon ground cumin
6 eggs, beaten
2 tablespoons whole or low-fat milk
Salt and freshly ground black pepper

You can't unscramble scrambled eggs.

—American proverb

Heat ½ tablespoon of the butter in a medium skillet until it foams. Add the red bell pepper, scallions, and optional green chile. Sauté over low heat until they have softened a bit. Toss the avocado dice with the lemon juice and add to the skillet mixture along with the cilantro or parsley, sour cream, and cumin. Cook, stirring, just until the mixture is heated through. Remove from the heat and cover.

Beat the eggs well with the milk and add a bit of salt and pepper. Heat the remaining butter in a nonstick Silverstone skillet. When hot enough to make a drop of water sizzle, pour in the eggs. As the eggs set, lift the sides with a spatula and tip the skillet to allow the uncooked eggs to run underneath. Do this until the eggs are set on top. Slide the eggs out onto a serving plate. Spread the avocado mixture over the eggs, then cut into 4 or 6 wedges to serve.

Serves 4 to 6

He who scrambles his eggs should not expect to eat them sunnyside up.

MIGAS (Scrambled Eggs with Tostados)

Migas literally means "crumbs" in Spanish, and this quick and excellent southwestern standard was developed as a way of using bits of stale, leftover tortillas.

2 tablespoons safflower oil
6 not-too-fresh corn tortillas, cut into
   1-inch squares
1 tablespoon butter
1 small onion, minced
1 clove garlic, minced
1 small green bell pepper, diced
2 medium ripe tomatoes, chopped
1 teaspoon ground cumin
Salt and freshly ground black pepper
6 eggs, well beaten
2 tablespoons whole or low-fat milk

Heat the oil in a large skillet. Add the tortilla pieces and sauté over moderate heat, stirring often, until they curl and look crisp. Transfer them to a plate.

In the same skillet, heat the butter until it foams. Add the onion and garlic and sauté over low heat until the onion is translucent. Add the green pepper and continue to sauté until the onion is golden. Add the tomatoes and sauté just until they have softened a bit. Stir in the tortilla pieces, then turn the heat up so that the skillet becomes very hot. Pour in the eggs, beaten with the milk. Scramble softly until the eggs are set. Serve at once.

Serves 4 to 6

BREAKFAST BURRITOS

I enjoyed Breakfast Burritos, which are basically scrambled eggs wrapped in soft flour tortillas, in several locales across the Southwest. I'd like to rename them Brunch Burritos, since I'm not quite ready for green chiles until 11:00 A.M.!

6 eggs, beaten
2 tablespoons whole or low-fat milk
Salt and freshly ground black pepper
1½ tablespoons butter
Eight 8-inch flour tortillas (page
   143), warmed
1 recipe Green Chile Sauce (page 149)
1 cup firmly packed grated Cheddar
   cheese

Preheat the oven to 350° F.

Beat the eggs well with the milk. Season with a bit of salt and pepper. Heat the butter in a large skillet until it foams. Pour in the eggs and scramble them until they are done. Distribute the eggs among the tortillas, arranging them in the center of each. Fold the tortillas as instructed in the illustration on page 142.

Place the burritos, seam side down, in a lightly oiled large, shallow baking dish. Spread the Green Chili Sauce evenly over the tops, then sprinkle them with the grated cheese. Bake for 15 to 20 minutes, or until the cheese is bubbly.

Serves 4

POTATO OMELET

Here is another great southwestern egg specialty in the form of a flat omelet, known as a *torta*. This omelet of potatoes and green chiles is a common one and is as simple as it is satisfying.

2 tablespoons safflower oil
1 medium onion, finely chopped
1 large potato, cooked in its skin, peeled and finely diced
One 4-ounce can mild or hot green chiles, drained and chopped
Salt and freshly ground black pepper
6 eggs, beaten
2 tablespoons whole or low-fat milk
½ cup grated Monterey Jack cheese
Salsa Ranchera (page 148)

Heat the safflower oil in a 10-inch nonstick Silverstone skillet. Add the onion and sauté over low heat until it is golden. Add the potato dice and continue to sauté for about 2 minutes. Stir in the green chiles and add a little salt and pepper. Sauté until everything is well heated through. Distribute the mixture evenly over the bottom of the skillet and turn the heat up to moderate.

Beat the eggs well with the milk. When the skillet is hot enough to make a drop of water sizzle, pour the eggs in. As the omelet begins to set, lift the sides with a spatula and tip the skillet to allow the uncooked eggs to run underneath. When the eggs are fairly set on top, sprinkle on the cheese and cover. Cook until the cheese is bubbly. Slide the omelet out onto a serving plate. Cut into 4 wedges to serve. Pass around some Salsa Ranchera for topping if you'd like.

Serves 4

CALIFORNIA OMELET

This is another simple flat omelet, or *torta,* nicely flavored with the standard "Spanish" seasonings.

1 tablespoon olive oil
1 medium onion, chopped
2 cloves garlic, minced
1 small green or red bell pepper, diced
1 cup chopped ripe tomatoes
One 4-ounce can mild or hot green chiles, drained and chopped
½ teaspoon dried oregano
Salt and freshly ground black pepper
6 eggs, beaten
2 tablespoons whole or low-fat milk
1 tablespoon butter

Heat the oil in a small skillet. Add the onion and garlic and sauté until the onion is translucent. Add the green or red pepper and sauté until it is tender-crisp and the onion is golden. Add the tomatoes, chiles, oregano, and salt and pepper and sauté until the tomatoes are soft and their liquid is reduced, about ten minutes. Remove from the heat.

Beat the eggs well with the milk. Stir into them the mixture from the skillet. Heat the butter in a 10-inch nonstick Silverstone skillet. When the skillet is hot enough to make a drop of water sizzle, pour in the egg mixture. When the omelet begins to set, lift the edges with a spatula and tip the skillet to allow the uncooked eggs to run underneath. When the omelet is firm, cover and cook until the top is completely set. Slide the omelet out onto a serving plate and cut into wedges to serve.

Serves 4

ARKANSAS BOILED-EGG PIE

A lovely and elegant pie, this makes a very nice dish for company.

1 tablespoon butter
1 medium onion, chopped
1 medium stalk celery, finely diced
2 tablespoons unbleached white
  flour
1 cup low-fat milk
1 cup grated Cheddar cheese
Salt and freshly ground black pepper
½ cup steamed fresh green peas or
  thawed frozen peas
One 9-inch piecrust (page 152)
4 or 5 hard-boiled eggs, sliced
Wheat germ
Paprika for topping

Preheat the oven to 350° F.

Heat the butter in a heavy saucepan until it foams. Add the onion and celery and cook over low heat until the onion is golden. Sprinkle in the flour and stir until it is well blended. Pour in the milk, ¼ cup at a time, stirring it in carefully to avoid lumping. When the milk is hot, sprinkle in the cheese and season with a bit of salt and pepper. Simmer over very low heat until the sauce has thickened, about 8 to 10 minutes, then stir in the peas. Remove from the heat and cover.

Prick the bottom of the piecrust with a fork in several places. Bake it for 10 minutes. When it comes out of the oven, line the bottom with half of the hard-boiled-egg slices. Pour over them half of the sauce. Repeat the layers, then top with a generous sprinkling of wheat germ and a dusting of paprika. Bake for 25 minutes. Let the pie set for 10 minutes or so, then cut it into wedges to serve.

Serves 6

There is a best way of doing everything, even if it be to boil an egg.

—Ralph Waldo Emerson (1803–1882)

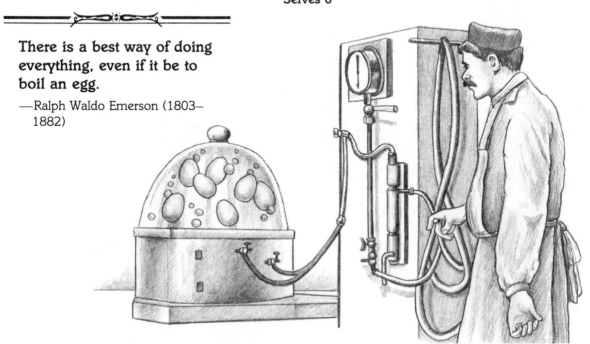

EGGS CREOLE

In old Creole cookbooks this preparation is likely to be called Spanish Eggs. It is a bit different, but certainly related, to the Spanish-influenced omelets of the Southwest. I encountered this as Eggs Creole at the Coffee Pot restaurant in New Orleans, so that will be its name here, too.

2 tablespoons butter
1 small red bell pepper, finely
    chopped
2 cups coarsely chopped
    mushrooms
2 to 3 bunches scallions, finely
    chopped
1 large firm, ripe tomato, chopped
¼ cup chopped fresh parsley
1 teaspoon paprika
Dash of dried thyme
Salt and freshly ground black pepper
6 eggs, well beaten

Heat the butter in a 10-inch nonstick Silverstone skillet until it foams. Add the red pepper, mushrooms, and scallions and sauté over moderately low heat, stirring until they all have softened, about 8 minutes. Add the remaining ingredients except the eggs and cook until the tomatoes are soft. Turn the heat up to moderate. When the skillet is hot enough to make a drop of the egg sizzle when tested, pour the eggs in. Let them set a bit, then scramble softly until they are done.

Serves 4

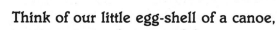

Think of our little egg-shell of a canoe, tossing across that great lake.

—Henry David Thoreau
The Maine Woods, 1862

EGGS NEW ORLEANS

This is another very nice Creole dish common to old New Orleans cookbooks. What make it special is that the eggs are broken whole over the sauce and baked.

2 tablespoons butter or safflower oil
1 small onion, finely chopped
1 large stalk celery, finely diced
1 small green bell pepper, finely
    chopped
2 cups chopped ripe tomatoes or
    one 14-ounce can imported
    tomatoes, drained and chopped
1 teaspoon paprika
¾ cup soft whole-grain bread
    crumbs
Salt and freshly ground black pepper
6 eggs
¾ cup grated mild white cheese of
    your choice
1½ tablespoons finely chopped
    fresh parsley

Preheat the oven to 325° F.

Heat the butter or oil in a medium skillet. Add the onion and celery and sauté over low heat until the onion is translucent. Add the green pepper and sauté until all are beginning to turn golden. Add the tomatoes and paprika and cook until the tomatoes are soft. Stir in the bread crumbs and season to taste with salt and pepper.

Transfer the mixture to an oiled large, shallow baking pan and spread evenly. Carefully break each egg, at even intervals, over the sauce. Sprinkle with the grated cheese and then with the parsley. Bake for 20 minutes, or until the eggs are set. Cut into squares to serve, making sure that everyone gets just one yolk.

Serves 6

Tew make a hen lay 2 eggs a day, reazon with her; if that dont dew, threaten to chastize her if she dont.

—Josh Billings
Josh Billings Farmers' Alminax,
1870

Chapter 6

CORN, BEANS, AND RICE

Most of the Inhabitants of America live solely on this corn, because it is very healthful and nourishing. For this reason they use it for baking and cooking, indeed for all things.

—William Byrd
Natural History of Virginia, 1737

for fritters

for stews

for baking

for elegant dishes

for puddings

The pivotal role played by corn in the development of American cookery has been mentioned several times in this book and can't be underestimated. Many of the recipes included here for utilizing corn are evolved from those that the American Indians taught the colonists. It is still the most abundant crop by weight in the United States.

Likewise, most of the varieties of beans used now can be traced back to the ancient South American Indians, whose knowledge traveled early to their North American counterparts. Robert Beverly said of the Indians in *The History and Present State of Virginia* (1705), "They eat all sorts of Pease, Beans, and other Pulse, both parched and boiled."

Rice came to us later, introduced to the young colony of South Carolina as a gift of seed from Madagascar. It soon became their major crop and staple food. By the early 1700s, rice had made its way to Louisiana, whose marshy lands were perfect for its cultivation. Louisiana eventually overtook South Carolina as a rice-growing state, and to this day, rice is a must on any true Creole table.

What is fascinating about these three staple crops is the regularity with which they've worked their way into nearly every regional cuisine (although potatoes become more widely used than rice as one goes further north, especially in the Pennsylvania Dutch and New England repertoires). Even more interesting is how the regional styles vary these basics, producing a seemingly endless variety of delicious dishes. I think, for example, of a typical meal I would sit down to in New Mexico—a plate of enchiladas, made with corn tortillas, accompanied by pinto beans and *arroz* (Mexican rice).

Then there are those wonderful southern dishes that instinctively combine beans or peas with rice, such as Hopping-John (black-eyed peas and rice), the Cuban-influenced Black Beans and Rice, and the New Orleans classic Red Beans and Rice. These were easy to adapt—the original recipes contained a small bit of meat for flavoring, and this was simply deleted, leaving a dish still packed with flavor and high in protein.

Almost every region, too, has its own brand of succotash, from which I chose three, amazingly varied and far more exotic than the plain corn and lima bean mixture we've grown accustomed to seeing in our supermarket's frozen-food section.

Corn, beans, and rice must have played at least as great a role in the diet of earlier Americans as they do in today's vegetarian diet. As grains and legumes, they are the backbone of our protein needs, just as they must have been in the earlier American diet, which did not become so meat-centered until the twentieth century. The imagination of the cooks of days past made building a chapter around these healthy and versatile staples a real pleasure.

CORN-STUFFED PEPPERS

This attractive recipe is quite common in old southern cookbooks. I suggest making this in the late summer, when it starts getting cool enough in the evenings to bake, using fresh sweet corn and a combination of both green and red bell peppers. This colorful preparation is an enticing dish for company.

6 green or red bell peppers or 3 of each
2 tablespoons butter
1 medium onion, chopped
2 teaspoons unbleached white flour
1 teaspoon paprika
¼ teaspoon dried thyme
A few grains cayenne pepper
⅔ cup whole or low-fat milk
3 cups cooked fresh corn kernels (3 to 4 ears)
2 to 3 tablespoons chopped fresh parsley
½ cup fine whole-grain bread crumbs
Salt and freshly ground black pepper
Additional bread crumbs for topping
Paprika for topping

Preheat the oven to 350° F.

Prepare the peppers by cutting off the stems and slicing them in half lengthwise. Remove the seeds and white membranes and arrange the halves, cut side up, in 1 or 2 oiled shallow baking pans.

In a deep, heavy saucepan, heat the butter until it foams. Add the onion and sauté over low heat until it is golden. Sprinkle in the flour, paprika, thyme, and cayenne and stir in until smoothly blended. Cook, stirring continuously, until the mixture begins to brown lightly. Pour in the milk, a little at a time, stirring carefully to ensure smoothness. Allow the mixture to simmer gently until it thickens, about 5 to 7 minutes.

Stir in the corn, parsley, and bread crumbs. Season to taste with salt and pepper and remove from the heat. Distribute the stuffing among the peppers. Top each one with a small amount of additional bread crumbs and a dusting of paprika.

Bake, covered, for 20 minutes, then uncover and bake another 10 to 15 minutes, or until the peppers are done to your liking.

Serves 6

And those who came were resolved
   to be Englishmen
Gone to the World's end,
   but English every one,
And they ate the white corn kernels
   parched in the sun,
And they knew it not,
   but they'd not be English again.

—Stephen Vincent Benet
"Western Star," 1943

SCALLOPED CORN

Scalloped corn is more of a general than a regional American recipe. I can imagine this simple but very delicious dish being served on the family tables of the Great Plains around the turn of the century.

1 tablespoon safflower oil
1 large onion, chopped
1 large green bell pepper, finely diced
2 medium firm, ripe tomatoes, chopped
1½ tablespoons unbleached white flour
¼ teaspoon paprika
A few grains cayenne pepper
1 cup whole or low-fat milk
3 cups cooked fresh corn kernels (3 to 4 ears)
Salt and freshly ground black pepper
1 tablespoon butter, melted
1 cup soft whole-grain bread crumbs

Preheat the oven to 350° F.

Heat the oil in a large skillet. Add the onion and sauté over low heat until it is golden. Add the green pepper and tomatoes and continue to sauté just until they soften. Sprinkle in the flour, paprika, and cayenne, stirring them in until well blended. Pour the milk in slowly, stirring continuously. Bring to just under the boiling point, then stir in the corn and simmer for another minute or so. Season to taste with salt and pepper.

Pour the mixture into an oiled shallow, oblong baking pan. Toss the melted butter with the bread crumbs until they are evenly coated and distribute the crumbs over the corn mixture. Bake for 25 minutes, or until the crumbs begin to turn crusty.

Serves 4 to 6

It is not elegant to gnaw Indian corn. The kernels should be scored with a knife, scraped off into the plate, and then eaten with a fork. Ladies should be particularly careful how they manage so ticklish a dainty, lest the exhibition rub off a little desirable romance.

—Charles Day
Hints on Etiquette, 1844

CORN PUDDING

Here is another classic American recipe, still very common in the South (but also known as an old New England recipe), that requires the freshest, sweetest corn to be at its optimal in flavor. I like using the sweet white corn of midsummer for this delicate, custardlike treat.

3 heaping cups cooked fresh corn
   kernels (about 4 medium ears)
3 eggs, well beaten
3 tablespoons unbleached white
   flour
1 teaspoon salt, or to taste
2 tablespoons butter, melted
1 cup whole milk

Preheat the oven to 325° F.

Take care not to overcook the corn. It should be just done. When it's cool enough to handle, scrape the kernels off with a sharp knife and place them in a mixing bowl. Add the eggs and sprinkle in the flour, stirring to blend. Add the salt, milk, and melted butter and mix together thoroughly.

Pour the mixture into an oiled 1½-quart baking casserole. Bake for about 1 hour, or until the top is golden brown and the pudding is set.

Serves 6 to 8

CORN OYSTERS

Corn Oysters, or as they were sometimes called, Mock Oysters, were thought to be so named because they fooled the unaware into thinking that they were real fried oysters. Perhaps this is just a far-fetched yarn, but in any case, this is an old and very common recipe with probable New England origins.

3 large ears fresh raw corn
1 large egg, well beaten
1 tablespoon milk
2 tablespoons unbleached white
   flour
Salt and freshly ground black pepper
Safflower oil for frying

Cut the whole corn kernels off the cobs with a sharp knife. Process them in the container of a food processor or blender, in batches if necessary, until the kernels are very finely minced.

Combine the corn pulp in a mixing bowl with the beaten egg and the milk. Sprinkle in the flour and season to taste with salt and pepper.

Heat just enough oil to coat the bottom of a nonstick Silverstone skillet. When it's hot enough to make a drop of water sizzle, drop the corn mixture into the skillet by heaping tablespoonfuls. Fry over moderately low heat on both sides until nicely browned and crisp. Drain on paper towels.

Makes about 16

NOTE: If you're in the thick of the corn season, you can easily double the recipe if you'd like to make a bigger batch.

PENNSYLVANIA DUTCH CORN NOODLES

Broad egg noodles are a well-known item from the Pennsylvania Dutch cuisine, and teamed with fresh corn and ripe tomatoes, this traditional treat makes a wonderful summer supper dish. The simple preparation will get you in and out of the kitchen very quickly. For a nontraditional variation, pass around some freshly grated Parmesan cheese to top each serving.

2 tablespoons butter
2 medium onions, chopped
3 heaping cups diced ripe, juicy
    tomatoes
¼ cup water
2 cups cooked fresh corn kernels
    (about 3 medium ears)
¼ cup chopped fresh parsley
½ pound egg noodles, cooked and
    hot
Salt and freshly ground black pepper
Grated Parmesan cheese for topping
    (optional)

Heat the butter in a large skillet until it foams. Add the onions and sauté over low heat until they are lightly browned. Add the tomatoes and water and sauté just until they soften a bit. Add the corn and parsley and simmer just until everything is well heated through.

Transfer the skillet mixture to a large serving bowl. Add the hot cooked noodles and season to taste with salt and lots of freshly ground black pepper. Serve at once, topping each serving with some grated Parmesan cheese if you'd like.

Serves 6

SOUTHERN SUCCOTASH

It's no surprise that the characteristic ingredient of this southern variety is okra.

2 tablespoons butter
1 medium onion, chopped
½ medium green or red bell pepper, finely chopped
2 cups sliced (½ inch thick) young okra
2 cups chopped juicy tomatoes
⅓ cup water
2 tablespoons cider vinegar
3 cups cooked fresh corn kernels
2 to 3 tablespoons chopped fresh parsley
Salt and freshly ground black pepper
Dash of ground nutmeg

Heat the butter in a deep, heavy saucepan or small Dutch oven until it foams. Add the onion and sauté until it is translucent. Add the green or red pepper and okra and sauté, stirring frequently for 5 minutes. Add the tomatoes, water, and vinegar; cover and simmer over low heat until the tomatoes are reduced to a loose sauce, about 10 to 12 minutes. Stir in the cooked corn kernels and parsley. Season to taste with salt, pepper, and nutmeg. Cover and cook over very low heat for another 5 minutes. Make sure there is enough liquid to keep everything nice and moist; add a bit more water if necessary.

Serves 6 to 8

DUTCH SUCCOTASH

The Pennsylvania Dutch variety of succotash seems to typify their cooking style—very filling and simply seasoned, but certainly not bland, with a pleasant combination of flavorful vegetables.

2 tablespoons butter or safflower oil
1 large onion, chopped
1 medium green bell pepper, diced
2 medium potatoes, cooked in their skin, peeled and diced
2 cups cooked fresh corn kernels (about 3 medium ears)
One 10-ounce package frozen baby lima beans, thawed
2 heaping cups chopped ripe tomatoes
1 teaspoon paprika
Salt and freshly ground black pepper

Heat the butter or oil in a large heavy saucepan or small Dutch oven. Add the onion and sauté over low heat until it is translucent. Add the green pepper and continue to sauté until the onion is lightly golden. Add all the remaining ingredients and simmer, covered, for 20 to 25 minutes over very low heat, stirring occasionally.

Serves 6 to 8

COLACHE (Southwestern Summer Succotash)

In this Old California variation of succotash, the bright mélange of the freshest corn and vegetables makes for a wonderful celebration of the summer harvest.

1½ cups string beans, cut into 1-inch pieces
2 tablespoons olive oil
1 large onion, chopped
2 cloves garlic, minced
3 cups fresh corn kernels (about 3 large ears)
1 heaping cup chopped ripe tomatoes
⅓ cup water
2 small yellow summer squashes, diced
1 fresh or canned, mild or hot green chile, minced
1 tablespoon cider vinegar
Salt and freshly ground black pepper

Spring and early summer brought an abundance of tender young pumpkins, green beans, sweet corn, which were flavored with onion, tomatoes and chiles. The m'sickquatash (succotash) of the American Indian improved by stewing in olive oil and seasoning, became the colache of old California. It was the traditional dish for the season.

—Ana Begue de Packman
 Early California Hospitality,
 1938

Steam the string beans until they are tender-crisp, about 10 to 12 minutes. Refresh under cold water until they stop steaming and set aside.

Heat the olive oil in a deep, heavy saucepan or Dutch oven. Add the onion and garlic and sauté over low heat until the onion is translucent. Add all the remaining ingredients, including the corn and string beans and stir together well. Cover and simmer over very low heat for 20 to 25 minutes, or until the corn and squash are just done. Add the steamed string beans and simmer for another 3 to 5 minutes.

Serves 6 or more

BAKED CHEESE GRITS

Grits are the coarsely ground, dried inner corn kernel whose hull has been soaked off. An important Indian contribution to American cookery, the hulled corn kernel has been known as hominy since early colonial times. In its dried, cracked form it was called small hominy, later known as grits. Somehow, grits have suffered from an image problem, having become known as a sort of "poorman's food." There is a lot of evidence to the contrary; I found recipes using grits in many of the nineteenth century's most widely used cookbooks, including those aimed at a more affluent audience. Those recipes underscored the versatility of grits, using them in breads, muffins, puddings, and as a supper dish to substitute for rice. Baked Cheese Grits is a Deep South recipe of utmost simplicity, yet it is as elegant and satisfying as a soufflé.

4 cups water
¾ cup uncooked grits
1 teaspoon salt
2 tablespoons butter, cut into bits
2 eggs, well beaten
2 tablespoons whole or low-fat milk
1½ cups firmly packed grated sharp
   Cheddar cheese
Freshly ground black pepper

Preheat the oven to 375° F.

Bring the water to a rolling boil in a deep, heavy saucepan. Pour the grits into the water in a thin, steady stream, stirring continuously to avoid lumping. Turn the heat down to very low, then cook, stirring, for a minute or two. Add the salt, then cover and cook for 25 to 30 minutes, or until the grits are done, stirring occasionally. Remove from the heat.

Stir the butter into the grits to melt. Add the eggs, milk, cheese, and a few grindings of pepper. Mix together thoroughly and pour into a well-oiled 1½-quart baking casserole. Bake for 45 to 50 minutes, or until the mixture is puffed and the top is golden and crusty.

Serves 6 to 8

Pray let me, an American, inform the gentleman, who seems ignorant of the matter, that Indian corn, take it all in all, is one of the most agreeable and wholesome grains in the world; that its green leaves roasted are a delicacy beyond expression; that samp, hominy, succatash and nokehock, made of it, are so many pleasing varieties; and that johny or hoecake, hot from the fire, is better than a Yorkshire muffin.

—Benjamin Franklin, in a 1765 letter

POSOLE (Spanish Hominy)

Whole hominy, or "big hominy," is the result of soaking corn kernels until their hulls come off and is certainly one of the "lost foods" of American history. Having been a widely used item in colonial times, today it is mainly used in the Southwest in a dish known as Posole. An Indian recipe embellished by Spanish seasonings, the dish usually consists of the hominy stewed with meat in a spicy base. For our purposes, I have, of course, deleted the meat, so that what remains is a very unusual side dish. Whole hominy, with its nice, chewy texture, is available in canned form in Spanish groceries and in some southwestern supermarkets.

2 tablespoons olive oil
1 large onion, chopped
1 large clove garlic, minced or
    crushed
1 large green bell pepper, diced
2 cups chopped ripe, juicy
    tomatoes, with ¼ cup water, or
    one 14-ounce can imported
    tomatoes with liquid, chopped
One 20-ounce can whole hominy,
    drained
1 to 2 teaspoons chile powder, to
    taste
1 teaspoon dried oregano
½ teaspoon ground cumin
Salt to taste

Heat the olive oil in a large skillet. Add the onion and sauté over low heat until it is translucent. Add the garlic and green pepper and sauté until the green pepper has softened a bit. Add the remaining ingredients, stir together well, and simmer, covered, over low heat for 25 minutes. If there is too much liquid in the skillet, cook, uncovered, for 5 more minutes or so, until it is reduced. Serve at once.

Makes 4 to 6 side servings

Homminy is an American dish, made of Indian corn, freed from the husks, boiled whole . . . until it becomes almost a pulp.

—John F. D. Smyth
Tour in the United States of America, 1784

RIO CORN PIE

This is a recipe of special savor adapted from Phyllis Hughes' *Pueblo Indian Cookbook*. It is a perfect example of a dish of native ingredients, influenced by Spanish seasonings.

2 tablespoons olive oil or safflower oil
1 medium onion, chopped
2 cloves garlic, minced
1 medium green or red bell pepper, diced
1 cup cooked fresh corn kernels or 1 cup frozen corn, thawed
2 cups cooked pinto beans
2 cups chopped ripe tomatoes or one 14-ounce can imported tomatoes, drained and chopped
2 teaspoons chile powder, or to taste, or ¼ teaspoon dried red pepper flakes
1 teaspoon dried oregano
½ teaspoon ground cumin
Salt
4 cups water
1 cup cornmeal
¾ cup grated Monterey Jack cheese

Preheat the oven to 375° F.

Heat the oil in a large skillet. Add the onion and sauté until it is translucent. Add the garlic and green or red pepper and sauté until the onion is golden brown. Add the corn kernels, pinto beans, tomatoes, chile powder or red pepper flakes, oregano, cumin, and salt to taste. Stir well and simmer for 10 to 15 minutes. Remove from the heat.

Bring the water to a rolling boil in a heavy saucepan or double boiler. Slowly pour the cornmeal into the water in a thin, steady stream, stirring continuously to avoid lumping. Add ½ teaspoon salt and cook over very low heat, covered, for 20 minutes. (If you're not using a double boiler, you might want to use two burner rings under the saucepan to avoid burning the cornmeal.)

Oil a 1½-quart baking casserole and line the bottom with half the cooked cornmeal. Pour over it the mixture from the skillet and sprinkle over that the grated cheese. Top with the remaining cornmeal, patting it in smoothly. Bake for 45 to 50 minutes, or until the cornmeal is golden brown and crusty.

Serves 4 to 6

Corn has been since ancient times the most esteemed crop of the North American Indians and so has been the subject of a series of deeply ingrained corn dances, which are performed by Pueblos even today. The dances address the growth of the corn, prayers for rain, and thanks for the harvest, and their performance, often open to the public, is usually the culmination of rituals that are held for several days prior.

FRIJOLES REFRITOS (Refried Pinto Beans)

It's hard to think of anything more basic to the southwestern cuisine than the beloved frijoles. A good helping of them on the side of the plate is a standard sight at lunch, dinner, and sometimes even breakfast. Here is a simple vegetarian preparation (they are often prepared with lard, so do ask if you have them in a restaurant). Serve these on the side of the southwestern egg dishes in chapter 5 or with any of the tortilla specialties in chapter 8 that don't involve beans.

1⅔ cups raw pinto beans (about 4 cups cooked)
1 large onion, chopped
2 tablespoons safflower oil
1 teaspoon salt
1 cup grated Monterey Jack cheese

Soak the beans overnight. Drain and rinse them and place them in a large soup pot or Dutch oven with plenty of fresh water. Add the onion and 1 tablespoon of the oil, bring to a boil, then cover and simmer over very low heat until the beans are tender, about 2 hours. A good test of the desired texture is to press a bean between the thumb and forefinger; if it feels soft and mealy, it is done. Drain and store the beans until they're needed.

When you are ready to "refry" the beans, heat the remaining oil in a very large skillet. Add the cooked pinto beans and fry over moderate heat, stirring frequently, for 10 minutes. Mash the beans coarsely with a mashing implement. Add the salt and cook, covered, another 10 minutes or so, adding small amounts of water until the beans have the consistency of a very thick sauce. Sprinkle in the cheese and cook, covered, for another 10 minutes.

Serves 6 to 8

That's the bean called pink, called frijole, called the Mexican strawberry.

—*This Week Magazine,* March 1949

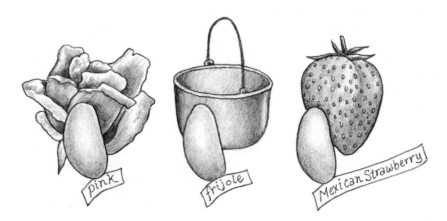

HEARTY RED BEAN CHILE

Perhaps the most exalted of all Tex-Mex inventions is the dish that has come to be known far and wide simply as chile (sometimes spelled "chili"). Originally Chile con Carne was a very simple stew of meat with green chiles. Later the stew evolved to include beans, spices, and sometimes vegetables. As chile cook-offs were held to determine who could make the most hair-raising or original chile, there seemed to be no end to the variations one could play on the theme.

2 tablespoons olive oil
2 medium onions, chopped
2 cloves garlic, minced
1 large green bell pepper, finely
    chopped
4 cups cooked kidney or red beans
One 28-ounce can imported
    tomatoes with liquid, chopped
1 or 2 jalapeño peppers, minced, or
    one 4-ounce can mild or hot
    green chiles, drained and
    chopped
1 teaspoon chile powder, or to taste
1 teaspoon dried oregano
½ teaspoon ground cumin, or to
    taste
Salt to taste
Grated sharp Cheddar cheese for
    topping (optional)
Hot cooked rice (optional)

Heat the oil in a very large skillet. Add the onion and garlic and sauté over low heat until the onion is translucent. Add the remaining ingredients except the salt and optional cheese. Simmer, with the cover just slightly ajar, for 30 minutes, stirring occasionally.

Remove ½ cup of the beans. Mash well and stir them back into the skillet. Add salt to taste and adjust the seasonings. Serve on its own in bowls, garnished with the Cheddar cheese, or over hot rice. On the side, you might like to have warm tortillas as well.

Serves 6

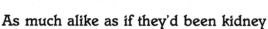

As much alike as if they'd been kidney beans, shelled out of the same pod.

—Ann S. Stephens
High Life in New York, 1844

RED BEANS AND RICE

If there were but one truly characteristic dish of New Orleans, it would be hard to come up with one more famous than Red Beans and Rice. A dish that has been around long enough to have become established in local folklore, it is also one that even today, graces many New Orleans restaurant menus. Vegetarians visiting New Orleans should be aware that "red and white," as it has come to be known, is most always made with a hot, smoked sausage. If you'd like to sample a meatless version, stop in at the I & I Creole Vegetarian Restaurant on Saint Peter Street and see if Amina DaDa, chef and owner, has made a batch that day. She adds a spoonful of peanut butter to impart a roasted flavor. That, along with a good dusting of cayenne, will produce an excellent adaptation of this classic.

2 cups uncooked red or kidney
   beans
1 tablespoon safflower oil
2 large onions, chopped
1 medium green bell pepper
2 large stalks celery, diced
2 cloves garlic, minced
1 cup canned imported tomatoes
   with liquid, chopped
2 small bay leaves
1 heaping tablespoon peanut butter
3 tablespoons chopped fresh parsley
2 tablespoons chopped fresh basil
   leaves or 2 teaspoons dried basil
½ teaspoon dried thyme
Salt and freshly ground black pepper
Cayenne pepper to taste
Hot cooked rice

Soak the beans overnight. When you're ready to cook them, drain and rinse them and place them in a soup pot or Dutch oven with water in approximately 1½ times their bulk. Bring to a boil and add the oil, onions, garlic, green pepper, celery, tomatoes, and bay leaves. Cover and simmer over low heat for 1 hour. At this point the water level should be just below the beans and vegetables. Add a bit more water if necessary to bring it to that level. Add the peanut butter and seasonings and simmer for another 1½ hours, stirring occasionally. At this point there should be a thick, saucelike consistency to the liquid. Mash a small amount of beans against the side of the pot with a wooden spoon. Cover and cook until the beans have burst and are very soft. It should have a thick, saucy texture. Remove the bay leaves. Serve over hot cooked rice.

Serves 6 to 8

Local lore on Red Beans and Rice tells us that to eat this dish on Monday was supposed to bring good luck. Conversely, the expression, "I am on the red and white," meant that one was broke.

FRIJOLES BORRACHOS

The word *borracho* was a nineteenth-century north-of-the-border term for a drunkard, and so the title of this recipe literally means "drunken pinto beans." Simmering the pintos in beer, along with the fresh cilantro, gives them a really special flavor. If cilantro is unavailable, use fresh parsley, although the effect won't be the same. This is an exceptional accompaniment to *Huevos Rancheros* (page 78).

1 tablespoon safflower oil
1 cup chopped ripe tomatoes or 1
    cup drained canned imported
    tomatoes
2 large bunches scallions, chopped
4 cups cooked pinto beans
½ cup beer
⅓ cup chopped fresh cilantro
1 jalapeño pepper, seeded and
    minced, or one 4-ounce can mild
    green chiles, chopped and
    drained
Salt to taste

Heat the oil in a large skillet. Add the tomatoes and scallions and sauté over moderately low heat for 2 minutes. Add the remaining ingredients and stir together, then simmer, covered, over low heat for 30 minutes. If there is too much liquid in the skillet at this time, cook, uncovered, until it thickens up a bit.

Serves 6 or more

NOTE: You may use the directions for cooking the pinto beans given in the previous recipe. Do all the steps up to the refrying. As for the chiles, use a jalapeño if you'd like some hotness to this dish. The mild chiles, however, will allow the flavor of the cilantro to be more prominent.

Next to rhy bread, beans hav been called by the poets, and philosophers the cumfort, and staff ov life. The bean iz all food, thare is no more waste in them, than thare iz in a pint ov cold water, when a man is auphull dry. Beans are all colors, and most shapes, flat, round, oblong, square and 3 cornered, and a quart ov them put in a pot, and biled 2 hours, will meazzure a gallon, and a haff, when they cum out. This makes them a better dividend paying seed than enny thing we kno ov.

—Josh Billings
   Old Probability, Perhaps Rain, Perhaps Not,
   1879

SPANISH-STYLE GARBANZOS

The garbanzo, or chick-pea, was one of the foods brought by the early Spanish settlers to the Southwest. This is a standard preparation—simple, but very aromatic and satisfying.

2 tablespoons olive oil
2 medium onions, chopped
3 cloves garlic, minced
3 cups cooked garbanzos
2 cups chopped ripe tomatoes, with
  ¼ cup water, or one 14-ounce
  can imported tomatoes with
  liquid, chopped
1 tablespoon minced cilantro
  (optional)
½ teaspoon dried oregano
½ teaspoon dried basil
¼ teaspoon ground cumin
Salt and freshly ground black pepper
Hot cooked rice

Heat the oil in a large skillet. Add the onions and sauté over low heat until they are translucent. Add the garlic and continue to sauté until the onion begins to turn golden. Add the garbanzos, tomatoes, optional cilantro, oregano, basil, and cumin. Cover and simmer over very low heat for 20 minutes, stirring once or twice. Season to taste with salt and lots of pepper.

Serve over hot cooked rice in bowls.

Serves 4 to 6

COWPEAS WITH CORN AND RICE

Cowpeas are small, brown, and tasty and bear a small dark spot on their sides, as does the black-eyed pea. Perhaps more closely related to the field pea, this little legume is known almost exclusively in the South, although I had no trouble finding them in dried form here in New York, where I live. This recipe comes from an old Louisiana family cookbook, another of that sort in which the matriarch sets down the recipes that her cook had undoubtedly known through oral tradition.

⅔ cup uncooked cowpeas
2 tablespoons safflower oil
1 large onion, chopped
2 cloves garlic, minced
1 small green bell pepper, diced
2 cups chopped ripe tomatoes, with
    ¼ cup water, or one 14-ounce
    can imported tomatoes with
    liquid, chopped
1 cup cooked fresh corn kernels or 1
    cup frozen kernels, thawed
¼ cup chopped fresh parsley
¼ teaspoon dried thyme
⅛ teaspoon cayenne pepper, or to
    taste
Salt and freshly ground black pepper
Hot cooked rice

Sort the peas and soak them overnight. Drain and rinse them and place them in a deep, heavy saucepan with plenty of fresh water. Cook until tender, 1½ to 2 hours. Drain and set aside.

Heat the oil in a large skillet. Add the onion and sauté until it is translucent. Add the garlic and continue to sauté until the onion is lightly golden. Add the green pepper and sauté for another minute or so. Add the cowpeas and all the remaining ingredients except the rice. Simmer over low heat, covered, for 15 to 20 minutes. Serve over hot cooked rice.

Serves 4 to 6

Mustn't pluck one's corn before it's ripe.

—Creole proverb

KEY WEST BLACK BEANS AND RICE

This dish has come to be known as a regional standard of Florida due to the popularization of black beans by the Cuban-American community. Once you have your cooked beans and rice on hand, this preparation requires a minimum of effort.

2½ tablespoons olive oil
2 medium onions, chopped
2 to 3 cloves garlic, minced
4 cups cooked black beans
2½ tablespoons cider vinegar
Salt and freshly ground black pepper
A few grains cayenne pepper
½ cup cooking liquid from beans
2 small green bell peppers or 1
    green and 1 red bell pepper, cut
    into julienne strips
Hot cooked rice
1 small onion, finely chopped

Heat 1½ tablespoons of the olive oil in a large skillet. Add the onions and sauté until they are translucent. Add the garlic and continue to sauté until the onion is golden. Add the beans, vinegar, and seasonings (lots of black pepper is great) along with the ½ cup cooking liquid from the beans. Simmer over very low heat, covered, for 15 minutes. With a slotted spoon, remove about ½ cup beans and mash, then stir well into the mixture. Make sure there is enough liquid to keep everything nice and moist but not soupy. Simmer, covered for another 15 minutes.

Heat the remaining olive oil in a small skillet. Sauté the bell peppers until they are tender-crisp and just beginning to be touched with brown.

Serve the black beans over a bed of cooked rice, topping each serving with some of the sautéed pepper strips and a sprinkling of the chopped raw onion.

Serves 6

SOUTHERN LIMA BEANS

Lima beans have long been, and are still, a much-used vegetable in the South. They are often called butter beans, and combining them with tomatoes, as in this Creole-influenced recipe, is a common way of preparing them.

1½ tablespoons safflower oil
1 medium onion, finely chopped
2 cloves garlic, minced
2 teaspoons unbleached white flour
1 medium green bell pepper, finely chopped
2 cups chopped ripe, juicy tomatoes
¼ cup water
4 cups (two 10-ounce packages) frozen baby lima beans, thawed
¼ cup chopped fresh parsley
½ teaspoon dried thyme
A few grains cayenne pepper
Salt and freshly ground black pepper
Hot cooked rice (optional)

The frost lies heavy on the palings, and tips with silver the tops of the butter-bean poles.

—George Bagby
The Old Virginia Gentleman,
1866

Heat the oil in a large skillet. Add the onion and sauté over low heat until it is translucent. Add the garlic and continue to sauté until the onion is golden. Sprinkle in the flour and stir it in until it "disappears." Add the green pepper and tomatoes and cook, covered, until the tomatoes have softened but are not mushy, about 8 to 10 minutes. Stir in the water, followed by the remaining ingredients. Cover and cook over very low heat for 15 minutes, stirring once or twice. Serve on its own as a side dish or over hot rice as a main dish.

Serves 6 to 8

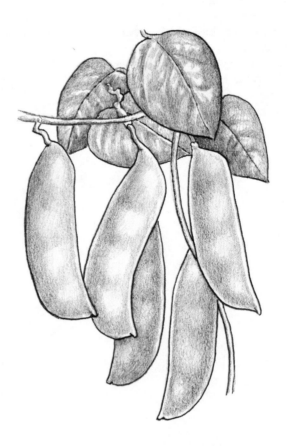

BAKED BARBECUE BEANS

A friend in Iowa recommended this recipe, noting that the contrast of the subtly sweet and tart flavors makes it a popular side dish at cookouts in his area.

1 tablespoon safflower oil
1 medium onion, chopped
2 cloves garlic, minced
1 cup thick tomato sauce
¼ cup molasses or light brown sugar
2 tablespoons cider vinegar
2 teaspoons Worcestershire sauce
1½ teaspoons dry mustard
1 teaspoon paprika
¼ teaspoon ground ginger
A few grains cayenne pepper
Salt to taste
4 to 4½ cups cooked navy beans

Preheat the oven to 325° F.

Heat the oil in a deep, heavy saucepan. Add the onion and sauté over low heat until it is translucent. Add the garlic and continue to sauté until the onion is lightly browned. Add the remaining ingredients except the beans and simmer for 10 minutes.

Combine the sauce with the beans in a 1½-quart baking casserole and mix well. Bake, covered, for 45 minutes, then for an additional 15 minutes, uncovered.

Serves 6

GREEN RICE

This traditional southern rice casserole, full of fresh parsley, makes a lovely buffet dish.

1 tablespoon safflower oil
1 large onion, finely chopped
1 large stalk celery, finely chopped
2 eggs, beaten
½ cup whole or low-fat milk
4 cups cooked brown rice
½ pound sharp Cheddar cheese, grated
2 tablespoons butter, melted
¾ cup firmly packed finely chopped
    fresh parsley
1 tablespoon chopped fresh basil or
    1 teaspoon dried basil
Salt and freshly ground black pepper

Preheat the oven to 350° F.

Heat the safflower oil in a small skillet. Add the onion and celery and sauté over a low heat until they are lightly browned. Transfer to a large mixing bowl and add all the remaining ingredients. Mix thoroughly, then pat the mixture into an oiled large, shallow baking dish. Bake for 35 to 40 minutes, or until the top of the casserole is lightly browned and the cheese is bubbly.

Serves 6 to 8

HOPPING-JOHN (Black-eyed Peas and Rice)

This is a famous Deep South dish, which in its original form always takes a piece of salt pork. It was traditionally eaten as a "good luck" dish on New Year's Day. My adaptation of this simple but delicious recipe is close to the Creole-influenced variety using tomatoes and herbs, thus adding flavors that more than make up for the absence of meat.

2 tablespoons safflower oil
1 cup chopped onions
1 clove garlic, minced
2 cups ripe, juicy tomatoes,
    chopped, with ¼ cup water, or
    one 14-ounce can imported
    tomatoes with liquid, chopped
½ teaspoon dried basil
¼ teaspoon dried thyme
3 cups cooked brown rice
2 cups cooked black-eyed peas
Salt and freshly ground black pepper

Now Hopping-John was F. Jasmine's very favorite food. She had always warned them to wave a pile of rice and peas before her nose when she was in her coffin, to make certain there was no mistake; for if a breath of like was left in her, she would sit up and eat, but if she smelled the Hopping-John, and did not stir, then they could nail down the coffin and be certain she was truly dead.

—Carson McCullers
A Member of the Wedding, 1946

Heat the oil in a very large skillet. Add the onions and sauté over low heat until translucent. Add the garlic and continue to sauté until the onions are golden. Add the tomatoes and herbs and cook until the tomatoes have softened a bit, about 5 minutes. Add the rice and peas and season to taste with salt and lots of pepper. Stir together well and simmer over low heat for 15 minutes. Add a bit of water or cooking liquid from the peas if the mixture needs more moisture. Serve at once.

Serves 4 to 6

RICE CROQUETTES

Rice, a major crop in Louisiana for over two hundred years, was a daily staple on the Creole table at nearly every meal. Even with the proliferation of outside cultural influences in New Orleans, the importance of rice in the local cuisine has not, to this day, been too much diminished. These croquettes, from an old Louisiana recipe, make a fine side dish.

2½ cups cooked brown rice
2 eggs, well beaten
2 tablespoons whole or low-fat milk
¼ cup finely minced celery
1 tablespoon grated onion
2 tablespoons minced fresh parsley
1 tablespoon minced fresh basil or 1
    teaspoon dried basil
⅓ cup fine whole-grain bread
    crumbs
Salt and freshly ground black pepper
A few grains cayenne pepper
Cornmeal for dredging
Safflower oil for frying

In a mixing bowl, combine all but the last 2 ingredients and mix thoroughly. Shape into small, palm-size croquettes (patiently, since the batter will be rather loose) and dredge in cornmeal. Heat just enough oil to coat the bottom of a nonstick Silverstone skillet. Fry the croquettes until golden brown on both sides.

Makes about 16 croquettes

BAKED RICE WITH CHEESE AND GREEN CHILES

In this southwestern casserole, the chiles and cilantro lend a marvelous flavor to an otherwise simple casserole. The more chiles, the better, but of course, tailor the amount and hotness to your taste.

1 tablespoon butter or safflower oil
1 medium onion, chopped
4 cups cooked brown rice
½ pound grated Monterey Jack cheese
1 cup sour cream
One or two 4-ounce cans mild or hot green chiles, drained and finely chopped
2 to 3 tablespoons minced cilantro (substitute parsley if necessary)
½ teaspoon chile powder
Salt and freshly ground black pepper

[The Indians] place their canoes close to the bunches of rice, in such position as to receive the grain when it falls.

—Jonathan Carver
Travels Through Interior Parts of North America, 1778

Preheat the oven to 350° F.

Heat the oil or butter in a small skillet. Add the onion and sauté over low heat until it is lightly browned.

In a mixing bowl, combine the onion with the rice and all the remaining ingredients. Stir together thoroughly. Pat the mixture into an oiled 1½-quart baking casserole. Bake for 35 minutes, or until the top is golden brown and bubbly.

Serves 4 to 6

MEXICAN RICE

Mexican Rice is the traditional accompaniment, along with Frijoles Refritos (page 97), to tortilla specialties of the Southwest. The secret of this savory rice is that it is fried in its raw state before the cooking water is added.

1 tablespoon olive oil
1 large onion, finely chopped
2 cloves garlic, minced
1 small green bell pepper, finely chopped
1 heaping cup chopped ripe tomatoes or 1 cup canned imported tomatoes, drained and chopped
1 teaspoon dried oregano
1 teaspoon ground cumin
¼ teaspoon dried red pepper flakes
Salt to taste
2 tablespoons safflower oil
1½ cups uncooked brown rice
3½ cups water

Heat the olive oil in a medium skillet. Add the onion and garlic and sauté over low heat until the onion is translucent. Add the green pepper, tomatoes, and seasonings and sauté until the tomatoes have softened into a loose sauce, about 10 minutes. Remove from heat and cover.

Heat the safflower oil in a large skillet (10 inches will be just adequate, 12 inches will be a bit more comfortable). Add the rice and sauté, stirring frequently, for 5 minutes. Add the sautéed vegetable mixture and the water. Stir together and cover tightly. Simmer over very low heat until the water is absorbed, about 45 minutes. Don't lift the lid during this time. At the end, check to see if the rice is adequately done. If so, toss the mixture together, as the vegetables will have risen to the top. If not, add another ½ cup water, and simmer, uncovered, until it is absorbed.

Serves 6

Chapter 7
VEGETABLES

We proceed to Roots and Vegetables—and the best cook cannot alter the first quality, they must be good, or the cook will be disappointed.

—Amelia Simmons
American Cookery, 1796

The advice given to cooks by Amelia Simmons, the author of the first American cookbook, could not be more on target, especially in today's world of processing, packaging, and importing. Most of the vegetable recipes I encountered from earlier days were not fancy or fussy, most likely because they relied on the good, basic flavor of the fresh produce. The majority of these recipes were developed in times when produce came straight from the kitchen-garden, or at the very least, fresh from a local market.

Colonial Virginia, from all accounts, was a veritable paradise of vegetables in quantity and variety, which are today difficult to imagine. Of great influence in introducing and promoting all manner of produce, and in elevating the home garden to an art form, was Thomas Jefferson. In the introduction to this book, I went into some detail about the lavish variety of vegetables commonly known in the early South. It seems safe to say, oddly, that nothing much happened (except perhaps a lot of regression) to the state of produce in America until the 1970s, when a resurgence of interest in unusual fresh vegetables seems to have been spurred by the popularity of ethnic cuisines.

When starting this project, I probably knew my way around the Oriental grocery blindfolded, but I had never worked with a traditional crop such as okra and couldn't tell a cymling from a mirliton. As far as I was concerned, parsnips were only for laughing at, and collard greens just looked like—well, too much trouble. Not that all the vegetables I encountered as typically American were this exotic to me—most were the old familiar standbys. There were plenty of white and sweet potatoes, cabbage, beets, eggplant, and several varieties of squash. The discovery lay not only in new ways of preparation, but more importantly, in gaining an awareness of a multitude of great winter vegetable recipes, many of which utilize the aforementioned items in interesting, satisfying ways. This should be especially cheering to those of us who miss the bright variety of summer and fall harvest goods, but still want to use what's fresh and in season during the cold-weather months.

The wide range of regional styles represented in this chapter hopefully reflects the knowledge and creativity of our earlier cooks—from the plain and hearty dishes of the frugal Pennsylvania Dutch to the lavishly seasoned improvisations of the Creoles, the American vegetable could not have been in better hands.

BEETS PIQUANTE

One of America's earliest cookbook writers, Mary Randolph, said in her 1824 book that beets "are not so much used as they deserve to be." I agree with this observation. I will grant, though, that they are not terribly versatile, they take a long time to cook, and that your kitchen will be splattered with reddish purple by the time you finish preparing them. Barring these minor obstacles, I was happy to learn two new and delicious ways of preparing beets, presented here on these two pages. This recipe is adapted from an old New Orleans cookbook.

6 medium beets
2 tablespoons butter
2 tablespoons unbleached white
    flour
¾ cup hot water
¼ cup light cream
3 tablespoons cider vinegar
2 tablespoons dry white or red wine
1½ teaspoons honey
¼ teaspoon salt
Freshly ground black pepper
A few grains cayenne pepper

Remove the green tops from the beets, leaving about ¼ inch of the stalks on the beets (save the greens for later use—cooked or steamed, they can be used like spinach and are very nutritious). Rinse the beets to remove loose dirt but take care not to break the fibers.

Bring a deep pot of water to a boil and gently drop the beets in. Cook over medium-low heat until they are just tender. This will take anywhere from 45 minutes to 1½ hours, depending on the size and age of the beets.

Drain the cooked beets and rinse them briefly in cold water. Trim the roots and tops and slip off the skins. Slice them ¼ inch thick.

In a large, heavy saucepan, heat the butter until it melts. Sprinkle in the flour and stir until smoothly blended. Continue to cook over low heat until the mixture just begins to brown. Mix together the hot water and cream and slowly pour it into the butter and flour mixture, stirring constantly to ensure smoothness. Bring to just below the boiling point, add the remaining ingredients and simmer gently for 5 minutes. Stir in the sliced beets and simmer over very low heat for 10 to 15 minutes. Serve at once.

Serves 6

HARVARD BEETS

Harvard Beets is a standard New England recipe, quite commonplace in the nineteenth century. I have modified the recipe by replacing the usual sugar-and-water mixture with orange juice, which enhances the beets' natural flavor without overpowering it.

6 medium beets
2 tablespoons butter
2 teaspoons cornstarch
3 tablespoons cider vinegar
⅔ cup fresh orange juice
2 teaspoons honey
¼ teaspoon salt
⅛ teaspoon freshly ground black
    pepper

Follow the directions for washing and cooking the beets given in the previous recipe. When they are done, slip off the skins and cut them into ½-inch dice. Set aside.

In a large, heavy saucepan, heat the butter until it foams. Sprinkle in the cornstarch until it is well blended. Stir in the vinegar, then slowly add the orange juice, stirring quickly to avoid lumps. Add the honey, salt, and pepper. Add the diced beets and stir together thoroughly. Cook over low heat for 20 minutes.

Serves 4 to 6

CREOLE EGGPLANT SOUFFLÉ

Eggplant is not a native American vegetable, but it is presumed to have arrived in colonial Virginia as part of the slave trade. Thomas Jefferson was an early proponent of eggplant, but it has failed to become part of any American cuisine, save for the Creole. Since the eggplant grew abundantly in the area of New Orleans and was sold in the famous French Market, Creole cooks developed some wonderful ways with it. Here are two worthy favorites, beginning with this flavorfully seasoned soufflé.

2 tablespoons butter
1 medium onion, finely chopped
1 medium stalk celery, finely diced
2 cloves garlic, minced
1 tablespoon unbleached white flour
2 tablespoons minced fresh parsley
1 tablespoon minced fresh basil or
½ teaspoon dried basil
½ teaspoon dried thyme
½ cup whole or low-fat milk
1 large eggplant (about 1½ pounds),
 peeled and diced
½ cup fresh, soft whole-grain bread
 crumbs
1 cup firmly packed grated mild
 white cheese of your choice
Salt and freshly ground black pepper
A few grains cayenne pepper
3 eggs, separated, at room
 temperature

Preheat the oven to 350° F.

In a large skillet, heat the butter until it foams. Add the onion, celery, and garlic and sauté over low heat until the onion is translucent. Sprinkle in the flour, stirring until well blended. Add the herbs and sauté, stirring until the mixture just begins to brown. Add the milk and the eggplant dice. Cover and cook over low heat, stirring occasionally, until the eggplant is quite tender. Add a bit of water from time to time if necessary, just enough to keep the bottom of the skillet moist. Remove from the heat.

Transfer the mixture to a mixing bowl. Add the bread crumbs, cheese, salt and pepper to taste, cayenne, and egg yolks. Beat the egg whites until they form stiff peaks, then fold them gently into the eggplant mixture. Pour the mixture into a well-oiled 1½-quart baking casserole or soufflé pan. Bake for 40 to 45 minutes, or until puffed and golden brown. Let the soufflé sit for 5 minutes, then serve at once.

Serves 4 to 6

CREOLE STUFFED EGGPLANT

This dish is still occasionally seen on restaurant menus in New Orleans but invariably contains some shellfish. Older recipes are nearly equally divided between the seafood version and those close to this completely vegetarian recipe.

2 tablespoons safflower oil
1 large onion, finely chopped
1 large stalk celery, finely diced
2 cloves garlic, minced
1 small green bell pepper, finely
    chopped
2 medium-small eggplants (about 1
    pound each)
1 heaping cup chopped ripe, juicy
    tomatoes (substitute canned
    imported tomatoes if necessary)
¼ cup chopped fresh parsley
1 tablespoon chopped fresh basil or
    ½ teaspoon dried basil
½ teaspoon dried thyme
Salt and freshly ground black pepper
Cayenne pepper to taste
½ cup dry whole-grain bread
    crumbs

Preheat the oven to 375° F.

Heat the oil in a large skillet. Add the onion, celery, and garlic and sauté over low heat until the onion is translucent. Add the green pepper and continue to sauté until the onion is golden.

In the meantime, stem the eggplants and cut them in half lengthwise. With a sharp knife, score each half several times lengthwise and across, carefully removing the pulp. Leave a sturdy shell of about ¼ inch all around.

Chop the eggplant pulp and add it to the skillet mixture along with all the remaining ingredients except the bread crumbs. Add a bit of water, just enough to keep the mixture moist. Simmer, covered, over low heat until the eggplant is tender, stirring occasionally. Stir in the bread crumbs.

Set the eggplant shells in an oiled shallow baking dish, which should be of a size that they can be securely propped up against each other. Stuff them, then bake for 30 to 40 minutes, or until the shells are tender but not collapsed.

Serves 4

CREOLE OKRA AND TOMATOES

I learned to love okra pickled or fried while traveling through the South, as well as when it is combined with tomatoes, as in this classic Creole recipe. The acidity of the tomatoes seems to cut that "slimy" texture that us Yankees are so wary of, so be adventurous and try it!

2 tablespoons safflower oil
2 cloves garlic, minced
1 pound fresh, young okra, cleaned, stemmed, and sliced ½ inch thick
1 pound ripe, juicy tomatoes
2 bunches scallions, both white and green parts, minced
2 tablespoons cider vinegar
1 tablespoon minced fresh basil or 1 teaspoon dried basil
½ teaspoon dried thyme
Dash of allspice or nutmeg
Salt and freshly ground black pepper
Hot cooked rice (optional)

Heat the oil in a large skillet. Add the garlic and sauté over low heat for just a minute or so. Add the okra and sauté, stirring frequently, for 5 minutes. Add the remaining ingredients and simmer, covered, for 15 to 20 minutes, stirring once or twice, or until the tomatoes are reduced to a loose sauce. If the mixture becomes too watery, simmer, uncovered, just until it thickens up a bit. Serve at once as a side dish or over hot cooked rice.

Serves 6

Never plant okra while standing. Always stoop and the plant will bear while still low.

—Louisiana husbandry folk belief

SCALLOPED CAULIFLOWER

Maria Parloa, one of America's best late-nineteenth-century cookbook authors, said of cauliflower in the 1887 edition of *Miss Parloa's Kitchen Companion* that, "This is a handsome and delicate vegetable. It is a pity that more people do not know how to cook it properly." Cauliflower has never been an integral part of any particular American cuisine, but it was one vegetable that lent itself very nicely to scalloping. A commonplace way of preparing vegetables in such old general American cookbooks as Miss Parloa's, scalloping comes close to being a culinary cliché, saved by the fact that it makes certain vegetables taste so good. This recipe is inspired by Miss Parloa's.

1 large head cauliflower
2 tablespoons butter
2 tablespoons unbleached white
    flour
1¼ cups whole or low-fat milk
½ teaspoon salt
Freshly ground black pepper
1 cup firmly packed grated mild
    white cheese
2 bunches scallions, minced
1 cup soft whole-grain bread crumbs
Paprika for topping

Preheat the oven to 350° F.

Break the cauliflower into smallish pieces and florets, a bit larger than bite-sized. Steam until tender-crisp, about 8 to 10 minutes, then refresh immediately under cold water until the cauliflower stops steaming. Drain well, then pile the cauliflower into an oiled large, shallow baking pan.

In a small saucepan, heat the butter until it foams. Sprinkle the flour in, a little at a time, stirring it in until well blended. Add the milk, about ¼ cup at a time, stirring it in carefully to avoid lumping. Add the salt and a few grindings of pepper. Simmer gently over low heat until the sauce thickens.

Pour the sauce over the cauliflower, then sprinkle on the grated cheese, followed by the scallions. Top with the bread crumbs and garnish with a dusting of paprika. Bake for 20 to 25 minutes, or until the cheese is melted and the crumbs are lightly browned.

Serves 6

A Most Handsome Vegetable

RED WINE CABBAGE

Cabbage was a crop brought to the New World by the European settlers and, because of its hardiness, was especially valued in the colder climates. In New England, and in the heartland settled by the German immigrants (better known as the Pennsylvania Dutch), cabbage was a highly esteemed staple vegetable. This invitingly aromatic dish is adapted from a Pennsylvania Dutch recipe, although versions of it appear in New England cookbooks as well.

1 tablespoon safflower oil
1 large onion, cut in half and thinly sliced
5 heaping cups coarsely chopped red cabbage
1 large sweet apple, peeled, cored, quartered, and thinly sliced
½ cup dry red wine
2 tablespoons cider vinegar
1 teaspoon honey
½ teaspoon salt
Freshly ground black pepper
1 tablespoon unbleached white flour

Heat the oil in a large, heavy saucepan or small Dutch oven. Add the onion and sauté over low heat until it is translucent. Add the cabbage and all the remaining ingredients except the flour. Stir together and cook over very low heat, covered, for 25 to 30 minutes, stirring occasionally, or until the cabbage is tender-crisp.

Sprinkle in the flour and stir it in completely. Simmer for another few minutes, uncovered, until the liquid in the pot has thickened a bit. Serve at once.

Serves 6 as a side dish

Cabbage: A familiar kitchen-garden vegetable about as large and as wise as a man's head.

—Ambrose Bierce
The Devil's Dictionary, 1906

4.6°

FARMER'S CABBAGE

This old New England recipe is a pleasant and very old-fashioned way of preparing cabbage. It is almost reminiscent of a hot cole slaw.

2 tablespoons butter
2 tablespoons unbleached white
 flour
1 cup whole or low-fat milk
2 teaspoons cider vinegar
½ teaspoon salt
Freshly ground black pepper to taste
4 cups firmly packed finely
 shredded white cabbage
1 small onion, grated
3 tablespoons minced fresh parsley
⅓ cup soft whole-grain bread
 crumbs
Paprika for topping

Preheat the oven to 350° F.

Heat 1 tablespoon of the butter in a small, heavy saucepan until it foams. Sprinkle in the flour and stir it in until it is well blended. Pour in the milk, ¼ cup at a time, stirring it in carefully. Add the vinegar, salt, and pepper and simmer gently over low heat until the sauce thickens, about 10 to 12 minutes.

In a mixing bowl, combine the cabbage, onion, and parsley. Pour the sauce over them and toss until thoroughly combined. Transfer the mixture to a lightly oiled 1½-quart baking casserole.

Melt the remaining tablespoon of butter and mix it with the bread crumbs until they are evenly moistened. Top the cabbage mixture with the crumbs and sprinkle with paprika. Bake for 35 to 40 minutes, or until the cabbage is just tender and the crumbs are golden brown. Let the casserole stand for 5 minutes before serving

Serves 4 to 6 as a side dish

4.6°

PARSNIP CROQUETTES

It took me a long time to decide whether or not to include a recipe with such a less-than-elegant name as this, but once I tried these Parsnip Croquettes, I was convinced. It's amazing that one can make such a delicacy out of those gnarled-looking roots. This recipe is further proof of the wonders that have been worked with winter vegetables in the Pennsylvania Dutch tradition.

1 pound parsnips, diced
1 egg, beaten
2½ tablespoons unbleached white
    flour
1 tablespoon whole or low-fat milk
1 tablespoon grated onion
Salt and freshly ground black pepper
Cornmeal for dredging
Safflower oil or butter for frying

Steam the diced parsnips in a heavy saucepan with ½ inch of water, covered, until they are tender, about 15 or 20 minutes. Drain the parsnips for several minutes in a colander, then transfer them to a mixing bowl.

Mash the parsnips well, then add to them the beaten egg, flour, milk, onion, and salt and pepper to taste. Mix together thoroughly and allow the mixture to cool to room temperature. If time allows, cover and chill it.

Shape the parsnip mixture into palm-sized croquettes (the mixture will be a bit sticky to work with, so flour your hands). Dredge them in cornmeal on both sides. Heat just enough oil or butter to coat the bottom of a nonstick Silverstone skillet. When nice and hot, fry the croquettes on both sides until golden brown.

Makes about 16

Folk who would rather starve than eat parsnips would make a sizeable army. . . . There is little excuse for eating plain boiled parsnips, and fried parsnips are none too tempting, but parsnip croquettes are the ugly duckling become a swan.

—Marjorie Kinnan Rawlings
Cross Creek Cookery, 1942

These toddlers once despised parsnips. But now that they've discovered parsnip croquettes, they actually fight over them.

POTATO-BREAD STUFFING

J. George Frederick, who in the 1930s wrote his recollections of growing up on a Pennsylvania Dutch farm, noted that, "The Dutch are a potato-loving people, and why not, when they can cook them so well." Potatoes were indeed a staple of their cookery, and it is perhaps in their cuisine that the white potato gets more play than in any other regional style. This hearty stuffing recalls Thanksgivings of days gone by. For our purposes, we need not stuff it into anything, but simply enjoy it as a side dish.

5 or 6 medium potatoes, cooked in
   their skins
1 cup whole or low-fat milk
4 slices whole-grain bread
2 tablespoons safflower oil
1 cup chopped onion
1 cup chopped celery
¼ cup finely chopped fresh parsley
3 eggs, beaten
Salt and freshly ground black pepper

Nineteenth-century American folk belief held potatoes in high esteem as cures for various ailments. Here are two examples:

A potato, carried in the pocket, will cure or prevent rheumatism.

A sore throat may be cured by wearing about the neck a stocking, in the toe of which a potato has been tied.

Preheat the oven to 350° F.

Once the cooked potatoes are cool enough to handle, peel them and place them in a large mixing bowl. Mash the potatoes with ½ cup of the milk. They do not have to be too finely mashed.

Cut the bread into ½-inch cubes. Place them in a small bowl and pour the remaining milk over them. Soak for several minutes.

In the meantime, heat the oil in a medium skillet. Add the onion and celery and sauté over low heat until the onion is lightly browned and the celery is tender.

Add the bread, onion, and celery mixture, the parsley and the beaten eggs to the mashed potatoes. Season to taste with salt and lots of pepper. Pour the mixture into a well-oiled 2-quart baking casserole. Bake for 50 to 60 minutes, or until the top is a nice crusty brown.

Serves 6 to 8

SWEET POTATO PONE

Sweet potatoes, an underused vegetable in this country, have long been a valued crop in the South, where their yield was plentiful even when grown in poor soil. The nutritious sweet potato has come to be best known for its use in such recipes as Candied Yams and Sweet Potato Pie, but in times past the preferred way of preparing them was simply to roast them in the ashes of the fireplace and eat them piping hot. Sweet Potato Pone is a very old Deep South recipe. *Pone* comes from an Indian dialect and means "a small oven loaf."

3 cups firmly packed grated peeled
   sweet potato
½ cup fresh orange juice
1 teaspoon grated orange rind
2 to 3 tablespoons molasses, to
   taste
2 eggs, beaten
2 tablespoons butter, melted
½ teaspoon ground ginger
½ teaspoon salt
Cinnamon for topping

Preheat the oven to 350° F.

If you are grating the sweet potato in a food processor, you will have to run the grated potato through for a second time, otherwise it will be too coarse and take too long to bake. A coarse hand grater will yield the right texture.

Combine all the ingredients in a large mixing bowl and stir together well. Pour into an oiled 1½-quart baking casserole. Bake for 20 minutes, covered, then for another 35 to 40 minutes uncovered, or until the outside begins to turn brown and crusty. Let it stand for 10 minutes before serving.

Serves 6

A 19th-century traveller in Mississippi recorded that he " . . . had a [sweet] potato pie for dessert and roasted potatoes were offered to him as a side dish, drank sweet potato coffee and sweet potato home brew, had his horse fed on sweet potatoes and sweet potato vines, and when he retired he slept on a mattress stuffed with sweet potato vines and dreamed that he was a sweet potato that someone was digging up."

—Frank Owsley
Plain Folk of the Old South, 1944

BAKED SWEET POTATOES AND APPLES

Although sweet potatoes were never as favored in the North as they were in the South, this simple dish is an old New England recipe. A nice and very "homey" dish for the winter, it is characteristically sweetened with maple syrup.

3 medium sweet potatoes, cooked in
    their skins, cooled and peeled
2 large apples
2 tablespoons butter
⅓ cup maple syrup
Cinnamon
Ground cloves
½ cup apple juice

Preheat the oven to 350° F.

Cut the cooked and peeled sweet potatoes into ½-inch slices. Peel and core the apples. Cut them into quarters, then slice them very thinly.

Oil a deep, 1½-quart baking casserole. Arrange in it half the sweet potato slices. Dot them with half the butter. Arrange half the apple slices over that and pour over them half the maple syrup. Sprinkle lightly with the cinnamon and cloves. Repeat the layers, then pour the apple juice over the top. Bake for 30 minutes, covered, then for another 10 minutes, uncovered.

Serves 4 to 6

PARSLEY-POTATO CROQUETTES

There's nothing very "regional" about this recipe, but it is one that I noticed in several general nineteenth-century American cookbooks, concluding that it must have been a fairly common way to prepare potatoes. These log-shaped croquettes are very pretty to look at and make for an elegant side dish.

4 cups cold well-mashed potatoes
1 tablespoon butter, melted
¼ cup whole or low-fat milk
Salt and freshly ground black pepper
Dash of nutmeg
¼ cup firmly packed finely chopped
    fresh parsley
1 egg, well beaten
Fine dry bread crumbs
Safflower oil for frying

In a mixing bowl, combine the mashed potatoes with the melted butter, milk, seasonings to taste, and parsley. Mix together well and shape into oblong "logs," about 3 inches long.

Dip each croquette in the beaten egg, then roll it in the bread crumbs. Heat just enough oil to keep the bottom of a nonstick Silverstone type skillet moist. Fry the croquettes, on moderately high heat, turning them on all sides until the outsides are browned and crisp. This has to be done rather gently and patiently so that they keep their shape—using a pair of tongs is helpful.

Replenish the oil as needed and drain the croquettes on paper towels.

Makes about 20 croquettes

POTATOES WITH COLLARD GREENS

You wouldn't know to look at them, but most members of the family of greens are an important source of calcium and have a significant amount of protein. Greens have long been one of the cornerstones of southern cookery and a prominent item in the "soul food" repertoire. Traveling around the South taught me that greens are still well liked and served often, but that it is almost unthinkable to cook them without the characteristic piece of salt pork or bacon. The owner of a diner in South Carolina and his two cooks had a pretty good laugh when I asked them how a vegetarian could prepare greens without using the meat. They stated emphatically that I couldn't—it just wouldn't be the same. Undaunted, I was determined to find a recipe for these nutritious vegetables that would be both meatless and tasty—this combination of potatoes and greens fits the bill nicely.

1 large bunch collard greens (about 1 pound)
3 medium potatoes, peeled and cut into ¼-inch dice
1 tablespoon safflower oil
½ cup water
½ pound spinach, washed, stemmed, and chopped
2 tablespoons cider vinegar
Salt and freshly ground black pepper
A few grains cayenne pepper
1 tablespoon butter
1 medium onion, finely chopped

Wash the collard greens carefully and trim off the thick part of the midribs. Chop them coarsely and combine them with the potato dice in a large, heavy saucepan or Dutch oven, along with the oil and water. Cook over low heat, covered, stirring occasionally, until the potatoes and greens are tender, about 20 to 30 minutes. Make sure that there is always just enough water to keep everything moist, but not soupy. Add the spinach, vinegar, salt and pepper to taste, and cayenne. Cover and steam until the spinach is wilted.

In a small skillet, heat the butter until it foams. Add the onion and sauté until it is lightly browned. Stir it into the potatoes and greens. Serve at once.

Serves 4 to 6

Only remember that, if a bushel of potatoes is shaken in a market-cart without springs to it, the small potatoes always get to the bottom.

—Oliver Wendell Holmes
The Autocrat of the Breakfast Table, 1858

POTATOES WITH GREEN CHILE

Potatoes are not a big part of the southwestern cuisine, but this tasty recipe is a fairly common one and needs a minimal amount of attention as it cooks.

3 tablespoons olive oil
1 large onion, chopped
1 or 2 cloves garlic, minced
4 or 5 medium potatoes, scrubbed
   and thinly sliced
½ cup water
One 4-ounce can mild or hot green
   chiles, drained and chopped
½ teaspoon ground cumin
Salt to taste

Heat the olive oil in a large, heavy skillet. Add the onion and sauté until it just begins to turn golden. Add the garlic and sauté for just a half a minute or so, then add the potatoes and water. Simmer, covered, until the potatoes are about half done. Add the remaining ingredients, plus additional water if necessary to keep the mixture moist. Simmer, covered, until the potatoes are tender.

Serves 4 to 6

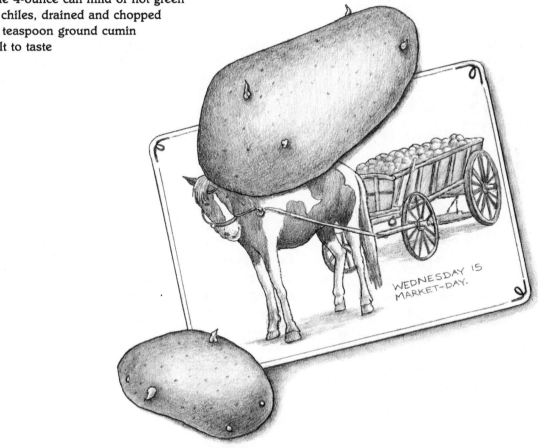

WEDNESDAY IS MARKET-DAY.

PECAN-STUFFED SQUASH

Squash and pecans, two favorite southern staples, make for a memorable dish when combined in this Louisiana recipe. The savory nut, bread, and rice stuffing, contrasted with the smooth sweetness of the butternut squash, will be a sure cure for the winter-vegetable doldrums.

2 medium-small butternut squashes
   (about 2 pounds each)
2½ tablespoons butter
1 large onion, finely chopped
1 cup soft whole-grain bread crumbs
1 cup cooked brown rice
1 cup packed finely ground pecans
⅓ cup orange juice, or as needed
2 teaspoons honey
Salt and freshly ground black pepper
Dash of nutmeg

Preheat the oven to 375° F.

Cut each squash in half lengthwise and remove the seeds and fibers. Cover with aluminum foil and place the halves faceup in oiled shallow baking dishes. Bake for 45 to 60 minutes, depending on the size of the squashes, or until the pulp can be easily scooped out with a spoon.

In the meantime, prepare the stuffing. Heat 1 tablespoon of the butter until it foams. Add the onion and sauté until it is golden brown. Combine the sautéed onion in a mixing bowl with the bread crumbs, rice, and ground pecans.

When the squash is done and cool enough to handle, scoop out the pulp, leaving a ½-inch shell all around. Add the pulp to the pecan mixture along with the remaining butter, stirring it in to melt. Add the orange juice, more or less as needed to make the mixture moist but not wet, and the honey. Season to taste with salt, pepper, and nutmeg, mix thoroughly, and stuff the squash shells. Bake for 15 minutes and serve at once.

Serves 4 as a hearty main dish or, when cut in half, 8 as a side dish

In Indian mythology, squash, along with corn and beans, is known as one of the three sisters. Often depicted as clothed in the leaves of the crops over which they are guardians, the sisters are also, in some legends, the daughters of the Earth Mother.

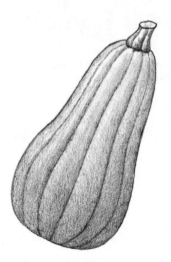

BUTTERNUT SQUASH SOUFFLÉ

Most of the squashes we know today were developed by the South American Indians and were already long in use by the North American Indians by the time the white settlers arrived. This abundant crop came to be especially favored in the South, since it continued to bear in hot weather. This soufflé, naturally sweet with the flavor of butternut squash, is a simple but elegant way to use this hardy vegetable in its season.

1 medium butternut squash (about 2½ pounds)
3 eggs, separated, at room temperature
⅓ cup whole or low-fat milk
½ teaspoon salt
¼ teaspoon cinnamon
⅛ teaspoon ground nutmeg or allspice
2½ tablespoons butter, melted

Preheat the oven to 375° F.

Cut the squash in half lengthwise. Remove the seeds and fibers. Cover with aluminum foil and place the halves, cut side up, in an oiled shallow baking pan. Bake for 45 to 60 minutes, or until quite tender. Remove the squash and reduce the oven temperature to 325°.

When the squash is cool enough to handle, scoop out all the pulp and place it in the container of a food processor or blender along with the egg yolks and milk. Process until smoothly pureed.

Transfer the puree to a mixing bowl and stir in the salt, spices, and half the melted butter. Beat the egg whites until they form stiff peaks. Gently fold them into the squash puree, then pour the mixture into an oiled 1½-quart baking casserole or soufflé dish. Drizzle the remaining melted butter over the top. Bake for 30 to 40 minutes, or until puffed and lightly browned.

Serves 6

squash   corn   beans

STUFFED MIRLITON

The mirliton is a small, green, pear-shaped squash that goes under different names depending on where you buy it. In the Southwest, it is called *chayote*, while in other areas, you might run across it as a "vegetable pear." In Creole cookery this pretty squash is well known as mirliton. This slightly modified version of a classic recipe (it usually contains seafood) was contributed by Amina DaDa, owner and chef at the I & I Creole Vegetarian Restaurant in New Orleans. For the adventurous, Amina recommends adding a bit of hiziki seaweed.

4 mirlitons
2 tablespoons safflower oil or butter
1 large onion, finely chopped
2 cloves garlic, minced
½ medium green bell pepper, finely chopped
2 tablespoons finely chopped parsley
1 small bay leaf
1 teaspoon dried basil
¼ teaspoon dried thyme
1 cup fresh whole-grain bread crumbs
Salt and freshly ground black pepper

Bring a large pot of water to a rolling boil. Drop the mirlitons in whole, cover, and simmer until they are easily pierced with a knife. This will take from 35 to 50 minutes, depending on their size. Once they are done, remove them from the water and set aside.

Preheat the oven to 350° F.

Heat the oil or butter in a medium skillet. Add the onion and sauté over low heat until it is translucent. Add the garlic and green pepper and continue to sauté until the onion just begins to turn golden. Stir in the bay leaf and herbs; remove from the heat and cover.

Cut each mirliton in half lengthwise and remove the seeds. Scoop out the pulp, leaving a shell of about ¼ inch all around. Chop the pulp finely and add it to the mixture in the skillet. Return to low heat, stir in half the bread crumbs, and season to taste with salt and pepper. Sauté the mixture just until the squash cooks down a bit so that it's not too watery. Remove the bay leaf.

Arrange the shells in a shallow baking pan; stuff them with the filling. Sprinkle the tops with the remaining bread crumbs. Bake for 20 to 25 minutes, or until the crumbs turn golden.

Serves 4

SIMPLE CYMLING RECIPES (Pattypan Squash)

The cymling, often called pattypan or white squash, is, I think, one of the most underused treasures of the American harvest, though it has been written of since the early 1700s. It bears closest resemblance to the zucchini in that it is quick-cooking and has a similar texture, yet its flavor is more delicate and delicious. The first time I asked my husband to buy some for me, I described it as looking like a pale-green flying saucer with scalloped edges. He had no trouble finding it. Making fussy recipes with the cymling would overshadow its lovely flavor, so I am presenting three very simple ways of preparing it. There's no need to peel the squash, but scrub it well.

I'll break that empty cymlin' of a head of yourn.

—Charles E. Craddock (a.k.a. Mary N. Murfree)
In the Tennessee Mountains, 1884

CYMLING FRITTERS

Cut 2 cymlings into ½-inch dice. Steam them until tender, about 10 to 15 minutes. Mash them well and stir together with a well-beaten egg and 3 tablespoons milk. Season to taste with salt and pepper. Drop by heaping tablespoonsful onto a lightly oiled or buttered nonstick skillet. Fry on both sides, over moderate heat, until golden brown.

BREADED CYMLING

Use 1 or 2 cymlings, as desired. Lay the cymling flat and cut it into ¼-inch-thick slices. Dip the slices first in well-beaten egg, then in fine dry bread crumbs lightly seasoned with salt and pepper. Fry in butter on each side, over moderate heat, until golden brown.

SAUTÉED CYMLING

This may seem too simple even to be considered a recipe, but it is perhaps the best way of all to appreciate the flavor of cymling. Use 1 or 2 cymlings, as desired. Lay them flat and cut them into ¼-inch-thick slices. Then cut the slices in half crosswise. Simply sauté the slices in butter, over moderate heat, stirring frequently, until they begin to brown lightly. Season to taste with salt and pepper and sprinkle with a pinch of mixed dried herbs if you'd like.

CALAVACITAS (Summer Squash with Corn)

This simple preparation is a traditional summer dish from the Southwest. The combination of fresh squash and corn, flavored with garlic and chiles, is absolutely delicious.

2 tablespoons safflower oil
1 medium onion, finely chopped
2 cloves garlic, minced
1½ pounds yellow summer squash, quartered lengthwise and sliced
¼ cup mild or hot canned green chiles, drained and finely chopped
1½ cups cooked fresh corn kernels (about 2 medium ears)
2 tablespoons chopped cilantro or fresh parsley
Salt and freshly ground black pepper

Heat the oil in a large skillet. Add the onion and sauté over moderately low heat until it is translucent. Add the garlic and continue to sauté until the onion begins to turn golden. Add the squash and chiles and sauté, stirring frequently, until the squash is tender-crisp, about 5 to 8 minutes. Stir in the corn kernels and cilantro or parsley and season to taste with salt and pepper. Sauté for another minute or two, then serve at once.

Serves 4 to 6

QUELITES (Greens with Pinto Beans)

Originally, this southwestern dish was made by the Pueblo Indians with wild greens. More contemporary recipes call for spinach or chard instead. The dark greens look very appealing with the pink beans, and the more garlicky you make it, the better.

1 pound spinach or Swiss chard
1½ tablespoons olive oil
2 or 3 cloves garlic, minced
3 bunches scallions, finely chopped
1 cup cooked pinto beans
1 teaspoon chile powder
Salt and freshly ground black pepper

Stem and wash the greens. If you're using chard, make sure to trim the thicker midribs as well. Steam the greens in a tightly covered pot until wilted—the spinach will be done as soon as it wilts, but the chard needs to steam longer; it will be done when it turns a dark green. Drain the greens and chop them finely.

Heat the oil in a large skillet. Add the garlic and sauté over low heat until it just begins to turn golden. Add the scallions and sauté until they soften a bit. Stir in the greens, beans, and seasonings. Cook, covered, over very low heat for 10 minutes.

Serves 4 to 6

EJOTES (Piquant String Beans)

This nippy preparation of string beans is adapted from the fascinating book on early Mission cooking of the Southwest, *Early California Hospitality* (1938). Use the youngest fresh string beans you can find for best results.

3 tablespoons olive oil
1 medium onion, finely chopped
2 cloves garlic, minced
1½ pounds string beans, trimmed
 and snapped in half
3 medium ripe, juicy tomatoes,
 chopped
1 or 2 jalapeño peppers, minced
¼ cup water
1 tablespoon cider vinegar
Salt and freshly ground black pepper

Heat the oil in a large skillet or a large, heavy saucepan. Add the onion and sauté until it is translucent. Add the garlic and string beans and sauté, stirring frequently, for 5 minutes. Add the remaining ingredients, cover, and simmer until the string beans are tender. This will take approximately 10 to 20 minutes, depending on the size and age of the string beans. Serve at once.

Serves 4 to 6

SIMPLE STRING BEAN RECIPES

String beans, also known as green beans and snap beans, have been a favorite southern garden vegetable for a very long time. The traditional way to cook them is in a big pot with a piece of salt pork—for hours. Although this method is still being used regularly, both at home and in restaurants, some younger cooks are devising lighter ways to prepare the ever-popular string bean. Here are two suggestions that I gleaned while traveling in the South. Of utmost importance is the quality of the string beans. Use them when their season is young, since no amount of effort will salvage the old and tough variety that seem to be on the market for the better part of the year.

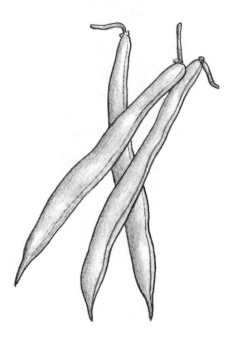

STRING BEANS WITH LEMON AND GARLIC

Trim 1 pound of string beans and cut them in half. Steam them until tender-crisp. In a large skillet, heat 2 tablespoons safflower oil and sauté 1 or 2 cloves garlic, minced, until golden. Add the steamed string beans and sauté, stirring continuously for just a minute or so. Remove from the heat, squeeze on as much fresh lemon juice as you'd like, and add a few grindings of black pepper.

Serves 4 to 6 as a side dish

STRING BEANS WITH TOMATOES AND BASIL

This preparation may sound rather Italian, but tomatoes and basil are a Creole combination as well. The somewhat smoky flavor produced by this combination might indeed be reminiscent of the deep, smoked flavor of salted meat.

Trim 1 pound string beans and cut them in half. Steam them until tender-crisp. Heat 2 tablespoons safflower oil in a large skillet. Add 2 large, very ripe chopped tomatoes and sauté them for a minute or so over low heat. Add as much chopped fresh basil as you'd like and cook until the tomatoes are soft. Finally, add the string beans, a dash of salt, and a few grindings of black pepper. Simmer over low heat for another 2 minutes.

Serves 4 to 6 as a side dish

SIMPLE TURNIP RECIPES

Turnips were a major southern crop for many decades and were as much valued for their nutritious green tops as for the root, if not more so. Turnips still show up on many a southern menu, often cooked with their greens and the ubiquitous piece of salt pork. I think turnips are an underutilized winter vegetable and lend themselves more to simple preparations rather than as part of elaborate recipes. Here are three very basic ideas adapted from the southern tradition.

From Jackson Square to the old French market is but a step. . . . If you enter the market now you will find yourself entangled in a crowd with whom you will be borne hither and thither, without any will or power of your own, through numerous stalls and a Babel of tongues. . . . On the left, beside her counter of vegetables, with potatoes and turnips arranged like cannon balls in an arsenal, is a rosy, rotund French dame, who invites you, with her blandest smile, to just step up and get good measure for your money.

—*Demorest's Monthly Magazine*
  "Stroll Through the Old Quarter
  of New Orleans," 1885

MASHED TURNIPS

Allow 1 medium turnip per serving. Pare and dice the turnips and steam them until tender. Mash them well, then sauté with a bit of butter in a nonstick skillet over moderately low heat until they cook down a bit (mashed turnips tend to be a bit watery otherwise, unlike mashed potatoes). Season to taste with salt and pepper. This is also delicious topped with bits of well-sautéed onion.

FRIED TURNIPS

Simply pare the turnips and slice them into ¼-inch-thick rounds. Sauté them in a little butter on both sides until nicely golden brown on both sides. This preparation gives the turnips a very pleasant, slightly sweet flavor.

TURNIPS WITH GREENS

Trim the stems and thick midribs of the turnip tops. Wash them well and chop them coarsely. Steam them in a covered pot until tender. Drain and chop them finely.

Pare the turnips and cut them into ½-inch dice. Sauté them in a little butter, stirring frequently, until they are golden brown on all sides. Stir in the greens and add about 1 teaspoon cider vinegar per turnip used. Season to taste with additional butter, if you'd like, and salt and pepper.

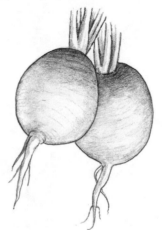

Chapter 8
SOUTHWESTERN TORTILLA SPECIALTIES

Tortillas were made by the Aztecs, long before Hernando Cortes looked down on the walls of Tenochtitlan. . . . The whole corn is first soaked in lime water and then boiled. The wet grains are crushed laboriously by pounding them with a stone on a *métate*—a rock mortar. The mash is then baked.

—Green Peyton
  San Antonio: City in the Sun, 1946

It's hard to imagine another region that keeps its culinary traditions alive more than the Southwest. Even more fortunately, the restaurant cooking seems closer to home cooking than in any other place I can think of. This feeling was echoed by several chefs and home cooks I spoke to. The backbone of this simple yet exotic cuisine is the humble tortilla—merely a flat disk of masa harina (limed cornmeal) and water, or of wheat flour, water, and a small amount of fat.

The tortilla was the staff of life in the early Southwest, just as bread was elsewhere. What is astonishing is the number of ways in which tortilla can be rolled, folded, stacked and shaped, with embellishments inside, outside, and on top. The best-known, and perhaps most traditional, are the enchilada (meaning, descriptively, "filled with chile") and the burrito (meaning, undescriptively, "little donkey"), from which all the variations seem to have evolved. I've concentrated mainly on these, rather than on the more elaborately shaped varieties, which involve deep frying—just too tricky for home cooking. But if you visit the Southwest, you might like to sample these innovations, such as flautas (tortillas rolled into flute shapes) or chalupas (bowl-shaped tortillas). You might also look for the blue tortilla, actually more of a gray-blue, that is made of blue cornmeal. These have a more nutty, distinct flavor.

One aspect of tortilla-based recipes that I particularly enjoy is the fact that most everything can be made ahead of time and then assembled at the last minute. This is very useful when cooking for company. Most sauces, fillings, relishes, and the tortillas themselves can be made in advance and stored until they are needed. Baking time, if any, is minimal—usually just long enough to melt the cheese, so there's little guesswork about when to put the food in the oven.

A bit distressing is the lack of general availability of good tortillas in areas other than the Southwest. Corn tortillas are generally available in frozen-food sections, but they are often disappointingly tasteless and dry. Wheat tortillas are even harder to find, but they, as well as better-quality corn tortillas, may be found in Spanish or Mexican groceries. Making tortillas by hand is somewhat tricky and requires patience, but I've included recipes for both, and the results make the extra time worth spending.

STACKED CHEESE ENCHILADAS

Few preparations are as basic to the southwestern cuisine as enchiladas, and as such, they have spawned countless variations and embellishments. Ana Begue de Packman, in *Early California Hospitality* (1938), explains that enchiladas, along with tamales, were the traditional food of the Mexican Indians. The Spanish colonists came along and improved them with their own special seasonings, as is the case with much of the food of the region. She also claims that the true enchilada is meatless. The word *enchilada* literally means "filled with chile," and so it is supposed to be drenched in pure, red chile. I've modified the recipe to use the tomato-based enchilada sauce, since working with the pure red chiles is not something that cooks outside the Southwest would be likely to attempt. This simple and hearty dish is traditionally enhanced by a helping of Frijoles Refritos (page 97) with Mexican Rice (page 109) on the side.

12 corn tortillas, as fresh as possible
1 recipe Cooked Enchilada Sauce
**   (page 146)**
½ cup finely minced onion
½ pound Cheddar or Monterey Jack
**   cheese, grated**
Shredded lettuce for garnish
Black olives for garnish

Preheat the oven to 350° F.

Place 1 tortilla on each of 4 or 6 ovenproof plates. Pour a bit of sauce over it, then sprinkle with the minced onion and grated cheese. Top with another tortilla and repeat the layers, once more for a 2-tortilla enchilada and twice for a 3-tortilla enchilada. Place the plates in the oven for 10 minutes, or just until the cheese melts. Allow the plates to cool a bit, then garnish with shredded lettuce and black olives.

Serves 4 to 6

When strolling through the southwest's older cities, the sight of ristras of chiles drying in the sun is a familiar one.

GREEN CHILE ENCHILADAS

This creamy, casserole-like preparation of enchiladas highlights the tendency of New Mexican cooking toward pure green chile as both seasoning and substance. Adding the zucchini is an unusual touch recommended by a friend from the region.

Filling:
2 tablespoons safflower or olive oil
1 small onion, chopped
1 clove garlic, minced
2 cups grated zucchini
1 cup (two 4-ounce cans) drained, chopped green chile
2 tablespoons finely minced cilantro
½ teaspoon dried oregano
Salt to taste

Sauce:
1¼ cups whole or low-fat milk
1 tablespoon butter
¼ teaspoon salt
2 tablespoons unbleached white flour

12 corn tortillas
1 heaping cup grated Cheddar or Monterey Jack cheese
1 bunch scallions, minced
Diced tomatoes and black olives for garnish

Preheat the oven to 350° F.

Heat the oil in a medium skillet. Add the onion and sauté until it is translucent. Add the garlic and continue to sauté until the onion is golden. Stir in the remaining filling ingredients and sauté, stirring frequently, until the zucchini is tender but not overdone. Remove from the heat and drain off any excess liquid.

In a small saucepan, heat the milk, butter, and salt until just under the boiling point. Dissolve the flour in just enough water to make a smooth, flowing paste. Whisk it into the milk in a steady stream. Allow the sauce to simmer until it has thickened, about 10 minutes, then remove from the heat.

Heat a heavy skillet and place in it one tortilla at a time for a few seconds on each side, just until it is flexible. If it seems very dry, sprinkle it with a few drops of water before heating. Place a small amount of the filling down the center of the tortilla, roll it up, and arrange it, seam side down, in an oiled large, shallow baking pan. Repeat with the remaining tortillas, placing them side by side.

Pour the white sauce evenly over the tortillas, sprinkle with the grated cheese, and top with the scallions. Bake for 15 minutes, or until the cheese is bubbly.

Serves 6

CHEESE ENCHILADAS WITH SALSA VERDE

With the distinctly flavored green to-matillo sauce, these simple enchiladas need little other embellishment.

12 corn tortillas
1½ cups sautéed chopped
    mushrooms, green and/or red bell
    pepper, yellow summer squash,
    or a combination
2 cups grated Monterey Jack cheese
1 recipe Salsa Verde (page 147)

Garnish:
Shredded lettuce
Chopped tomatoes
Black Olives

Preheat the oven to 350° F.

Heat the tortillas, one at a time, on a hot, dry skillet until they soften. If they seem particularly dry, sprinkle with a few drops of water before heating. Spoon a small amount of the filling down the center of the tortilla, followed by a light sprinkling of the cheese. Fold one edge over the other and place, seam side down, in a lightly oiled large, shallow baking pan. Repeat with the remaining tortillas. Spoon the sauce evenly over them and top with any remaining grated cheese. Bake for 10 to 15 minutes, or until the cheese is bubbly. Arrange 2 or 3 enchiladas on each plate and garnish with the lettuce, tomatoes, and olives.

Serves 4 to 6

GUACAMOLE ENCHILADAS

I found these enchiladas quite frequently on my travels, and it's easy to see why this rich, sensuous standard is so popular.

12 corn tortillas
1 recipe Guacamole (page 147)
Cooked Enchilada Sauce (page 146)
    or Green Chile Sauce (page 149)
1½ cups grated Monterey Jack
    cheese
Shredded lettuce
Diced ripe tomatoes
Sour cream or a mixture of half sour
    cream and half yogurt

Preheat the oven to 350° F.

Heat each tortilla in a dry, heavy skillet for a few seconds on each side until it is flexible. If the tortilla seems dry, sprinkle it with a few drops of water before heating. Spoon some guacamole down the center of the tortilla and place it, seam side down, in an oiled large, shallow baking pan. Repeat with each tortilla, arranging them side by side. Spoon any leftover guacamole over the top. Pour the sauce of your choice over the top, then sprinkle with the cheese. Bake for 15 minutes, or until the cheese is bubbly.

Garnish with lettuce and tomatoes and pass around the sour cream or sour-cream-and-yogurt mixture to spoon over the enchiladas, if you'd like.

Serves 6

BLACK BEAN TOSTADAS

Tostadas are crisp corn tortillas layered with a variety of tasty things. I still haven't figured out how to eat a tostada in polite company, but it is easiest to just pick the whole thing up as if it's a slice of pizza. In this particular case, the sour cream will end up on your face and the black bean sauce will ooze down your fingers, but if you're willing to forgo cosmopolitan propriety, you will have a sensuously good time. This delicious recipe, which I just couldn't wait to make after returning home from the Southwest, was contributed by Barbara Freer, owner of the Mainstreet Bakery in Taos.

1½ tablespoons safflower or olive
　oil
1 medium onion, chopped
2 cloves garlic, crushed or minced
3 cups cooked black beans
½ cup cooking liquid from the
　beans
1 teaspoon dried oregano
1 teaspoon ground cumin
Salt to taste
Safflower oil for frying
6 to 8 corn tortillas
1 recipe Green Chile Sauce (page
　149)
Grated Cheddar cheese
Chopped lettuce
1 or 2 medium ripe tomatoes,
　chopped
1 cup sour cream or a mixture of
　half sour cream and half yogurt

Heat the 1½ tablespoons oil in a large skillet. Add the onion and sauté over low heat until it is translucent. Add the garlic and continue to sauté until the onion is golden. Add the beans, liquid, oregano, cumin, and salt and simmer, covered, over low heat for 20 to 25 minutes. Stir occasionally and make sure that there is always enough liquid to keep everything moist and bubbling.

In the meantime, prepare the tortillas. Heat ¼ inch of safflower oil in a heavy skillet. When the oil is very hot, fry each of the tortillas, one at a time, over moderate heat, on both sides until crisp. This will require only several seconds of frying. Drain the tortillas on paper towels.

Arrange 1 tortilla on each dinner plate. Spread a bit of the black-bean mixture over each, followed by a spoonful or two of the Green Chile Sauce. Sprinkle on some grated cheese, then arrange over that some chopped lettuce and tomatoes. Finally, top everything with a dollop of sour cream or the sour-cream-and-yogurt mixture. Be generous with the layers, but not overly so, as the tostada must be bitable. Serve at once.

Makes 6 to 8 tostadas

If a yankee eats a tostado, he must hold a large plate beneath it, to protect his clothes.

CHILAQUILES (Tortilla Casserole)

In traditional American cookery, nothing was wasted. In many regions, stale bread became crunchy crumbs, perhaps for scalloping vegetables, or was cut into bits to make surprisingly sumptuous bread puddings. Similarly, stale tortillas go into making tasty Southwestern specialties such as Migas (page 81) or this unusual casserole, which I think of as a sort of Mexican lasagna.

2 tablespoons olive oil
1 large onion, chopped
2 cloves garlic, minced
One 28-ounce can imported
  tomatoes with liquid, chopped
One 4-ounce can mild or hot green
  chiles, drained and finely
  chopped
2 tablespoons chopped cilantro or
  fresh parsley
1 teaspoon dried oregano
½ teaspoon ground cumin
Salt and freshly ground black pepper
12 corn tortillas, not too fresh
½ pound Monterey Jack cheese,
  grated
Sour cream or yogurt for garnish
  (optional)

Full stomach, happy heart.
—Southwestern Spanish proverb

Preheat the oven to 350° F.

Heat the oil in a heavy saucepan. Add the onion and garlic and sauté over low heat until the onion is golden. Add the tomatoes, chiles, and seasonings. Simmer over low heat, with the cover on but slightly ajar, for 15 minutes.

In the meantime, pile the tortillas on a cookie sheet and bake them for about 15 minutes, or until they are dried out and rather crisp. When they are cool enough to handle, break them into several pieces.

Oil a large, shallow baking dish. Pile in half of the tortilla bits, then pour half the sauce over them. Sprinkle with half the grated cheese. Repeat. Bake for 20 to 25 minutes, or until the cheese is bubbly. Let cool for 5 minutes; cut into squares to serve. Garnish each serving with a small dollop of sour cream or yogurt if desired.

Serves 6

BEAN BURRITOS

Burritos, literally meaning "little donkeys," are a staple of basic Southwestern cookery; they and their variations are characterized by the use of flour tortillas. You can prepare burritos by simply wrapping around leftover *Frijoles Refritos,* but the filling presented here incorporates several savory flavors.

Filling:
2 tablespoons safflower oil
1 small onion, chopped
1 clove garlic, minced
½ medium green bell pepper, finely chopped
2½ cups cooked pinto beans
One 4-ounce can mild green chiles, drained and chopped
2 tablespoons chopped cilantro or fresh parsley
1 teaspoon cumin
Salt to taste

Eight 8-inch Flour Tortillas (page 143)
1 cup firmly packed grated Monterey Jack or Cheddar cheese
Salsa Ranchera (page 148)
1 cup sour cream or a mixture of half sour cream and half yogurt
Shredded lettuce for garnish
Black olives for garnish

Heat the oil in a medium skillet. Add the onion and sauté until it is translucent. Add the garlic and sauté another minute before adding the green pepper. Continue to sauté until the onion is lightly golden. Add the pinto beans, along with the remaining filling ingredients and enough water to keep the mixture moist. Simmer, covered, for 10 minutes. With a mashing implement, mash about half the beans. Make sure there is enough liquid in the mixture to form a thick, saucy base. Cook, covered, for another 5 minutes.

Divide the bean mixture among the 8 flour tortillas, placing the mixture in the center of each. Sprinkle with the grated cheese and fold the burrito as directed in the illustration below (this being a case where one picture is worth a thousand words). Arrange 2 burritos on each dinner plate. Spoon some Salsa Ranchera and sour cream over each one and garnish with shredded lettuce and black olives. Pass around extra salsa. Serve at once.

Serves 4

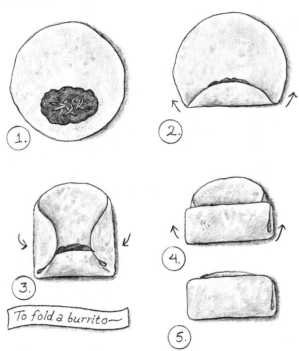

1.

2.

3.

To fold a burrito—

4.

5.

CHIMICHANGAS (Fried Burritos)

Chimichanga is a nonsense word very much akin to "thingamajig," and that's how this popular variation of burritos has come to be known. I've modified the procedure from the traditional deep frying to shallow frying with little oil.

**Leftover Frijoles Refritos (page 97—
   about half a recipe is needed)**
**Eight 8-inch Flour Tortillas (page
   143)**
1 cup grated Cheddar cheese
Safflower oil for frying

Garnish:
Guacamole (page 147)
Salsa Ranchera (page 148)
Shredded lettuce
Diced tomatoes

*Que vivan—que vivan
Los burritos para las bonitas!*

**Long live, long live
The little donkeys for the little
beauties!**

—Old California vendors' street cry
   Early California Hospitality, 1938

Divide the frijoles among the tortillas, placing a bit of the mixture in the center of each. Sprinkle the cheese over the bean mixture and fold the tortillas as directed in the illustration in the previous recipe, as for burritos. Secure the folds with 2 or 3 toothpicks.

Heat just enough oil to coat the bottom of a heavy skillet. Fry each chimichanga on both sides until golden brown and crisp. Arrange 2 on each serving plate and spoon a bit of guacamole and salsa on top. Garnish with lettuce and tomatoes and pass around extra guacamole and salsa. Serve at once.

Serves 4

Legend has it that Calamity Jane was awfully fond of burritos and chimichangas.

AVOCADO QUESADILLAS (Grilled Turnovers)

This is one of the popular flour-tortilla concoctions that I picked up while in New Mexico, and it's become a favorite of mine. It's slightly offbeat, but every bit as delicious as any of the old standards.

**4 or 6 unbaked 8-inch Flour
  Tortillas (see below)
1 large ripe avocado, finely diced
1 cup grated Monterey Jack cheese
2 or 3 bunches scallions, minced
Salsa Ranchera (page 148) or Salsa
  Verde (page 147)
Sour cream or a mixture of half sour
  cream and half yogurt (optional)
Shredded lettuce for garnish**

Prepare the flour tortillas according to the recipe, up to the point of baking on the griddle. Spread the tortillas out flat, dividing the avocado dice, grated cheese, and scallions among them. Arrange the filling on half of each tortilla, leaving about a ½-inch border near the edges. Fold the tortillas over and press the edges with the tines of a fork.

Grill each quesadilla on a hot, dry griddle or skillet on both sides until nicely golden brown. Arrange one quesadilla on each serving plate and spread with a bit of the salsa of your choice. Pass around extra salsa and the optional sour cream.

Seves 4 to 6

FLOUR TORTILLAS

Making these wheat-flour tortillas requires some patience. They are not as readily available as corn tortillas, and when they are, vegetarians must be aware that some ready-made flour tortillas are made with lard. The added benefit of this homemade recipe is the addition of whole wheat flour.

**1¼ cups whole wheat flour
¾ cup unbleached white flour
½ teaspoon salt
¼ cup vegetable shortening
About ½ cup warm water**

Combine the flours and salt in a mixing bowl. Work the shortening in with a pastry blender or the tines of a fork until the mixture resembles a coarse meal. Add enough water to form a soft dough. Turn the dough out onto a floured board; knead for a few minutes until elastic.

Divide the dough into 8 parts. Shape into balls and place them in a covered bowl to keep from drying out. Roll each ball of dough out with a rolling pin on the floured board to an 8-inch circle. Stack between sheets of wax paper or plastic wrap.

Bake each tortilla on a hot, dry skillet or griddle for about 30 seconds on each side. The surface of the tortilla should be lightly speckled with brown when done. Keep the tortillas wrapped in a towel as the others are baking. These are best used immediately, but if you'd like to save them for later use, wrap them first in foil and then in a plastic bag to store.

Makes 8 tortillas

CORN TORTILLAS

Despite the fact that making a dozen corn tortillas is somewhat of a production, I finally decided to include a recipe. These are better than their store-bought counterparts, with a fresher taste and a less brittle texture. The process is substantially easier with a tortilla press—hand rolling is tricky. Masa harina (limed cornmeal) is available in Mexican specialty groceries and also in some supermarkets, marketed by Quaker Oats.

2 cups masa harina
1¼ cups lukewarm water

Combine the masa and water in a mixing bowl and work together with your hands until the mixture holds together as a stiff dough. Divide into 12 parts and shape into balls. Place them in a covered bowl to keep them from drying.

To roll by hand: Place each ball between 2 sheets of wax paper or plastic wrap. Roll out, with a rolling pin, very carefully, into a 5- to 6-inch circle. Peel away the wax paper gently and trim the edges of the tortilla with a knife (you can probably make an extra tortilla with the excess that you trim).

To make in a tortilla press: Place a ball of dough between 2 sheets of wax paper or plastic wrap. Place on the bottom of a tortilla press. Press down with the top half of the press.

Keep the tortillas stacked between the wax paper or plastic as they are being individually heated. Bake each tortilla on a hot, dry skillet for about 45 seconds on each side. Keep the baked tortillas wrapped in a towel until they are all done. Use immediately or allow to cool while wrapped, then unwrap and store in a plastic bag.

Makes 12 tortillas

NACHOS WITH CHILE CON QUESO

A popular appetizer in the Southwest, this is an enticing, rich dish of melted cheese with chiles atop crisp bits of tortilla. Though this is customarily made with jalapeños, you can substitute mild green chiles to taste if you prefer a milder flavor.

12 corn tortillas
1 tablespoon butter
1 small onion, minced
1 clove garlic, minced
1 medium ripe tomato, finely
    chopped
1 or 2 jalapeño peppers, to taste,
    seeded and minced or sliced
1 tablespoon unbleached white flour
3 tablespoons milk
½ teaspoon salt
½ pound Cheddar cheese, diced

Preheat the oven to 375° F.

Cut the tortillas into quarters and spread them on 1 or 2 large cookie sheets. Bake for 15 to 20 minutes, or until they are dry and crisp. Remove and allow to cool.

Heat the butter in a heavy saucepan until it foams. Add the onion and garlic and sauté over low heat until they are golden. Add the chopped tomato and jalapeños and simmer until the tomato is soft. Sprinkle in the flour until it is well blended, then stir in the milk and salt. Add the cheese and cook, stirring, until it is smoothly melted. Remove from the heat and allow the mixture to cool for 5 minutes. Spread over the nachos and serve warm.

Serves 6 to 8

The origins of chile peppers are often credited to the South American Indians, whose formula eventually was adopted by the Indians of the Southwest. Chiles have since grown to be a big business— according to a recent report in the *Taos News*, chile is New Mexico's major vegetable crop, with nearly fifteen-thousand acres cultivated. This makes red and green chile a multimillion-dollar industry—that's a lot of hot stuff!

COOKED ENCHILADA SAUCE

Cooked tomato-based sauces such as this one are more common in some parts of the Southwest than in others. It's a good bet for those of you who are a bit shy of super-hot chile sauces, since it's milder and has a more familiar flavor. The seasonings here are those known as the Spanish seasonings.

1½ tablespoons olive oil
1 small onion, finely chopped
1 clove garlic, minced
½ medium green bell pepper, minced
2 cups chopped ripe, juicy tomatoes or one 14-ounce can imported tomatoes, lightly drained
½ cup thick tomato sauce
1 to 2 tablespoons minced cilantro or fresh parsley
1 small jalapeño pepper, seeded and minced (optional)
1 teaspoon good chile powder, or to taste
½ teaspoon each: salt, dried oregano, and ground cumin

Heat the oil in a deep, heavy saucepan. Add the onion and garlic and sauté over moderately low heat until the onion is translucent. Add the green pepper and continue to sauté for another minute or so. Add all the remaining ingredients and simmer over very low heat, covered, for 25 to 30 minutes.

Makes about 2 cups

Chile, or chilly, as the name of a sauce, and a very familiar word at this season, is in none of the dictionaries.

—*American Notes and Queries VII*, 1891

Not one of these dictionaries contains —
Chile sauce n.: a spiced tomato sauce orig. made with chilies.

GUACAMOLE

It's not easy to categorize Guacamole, since it is as much a relish as it is a salad. This recipe was contributed by a friend who grew up in San Antonio; he gives it a very special touch by roasting the tomatoes and bell peppers, imparting a subtly smoked taste.

1 medium firm, ripe tomato
1 small green bell pepper
2 large, very ripe avocados
Juice of ½ lemon
1 clove garlic, crushed (optional)
2 tablespoons finely minced cilantro
   or fresh parsley
½ teaspoon ground cumin
Salt and freshly ground black pepper
1 tomatillo, finely chopped, (optional)

Roast the tomato and green pepper under a broiler. Turn on all sides until the skins are quite blistered. Let them cool in a paper bag.

In the meantime, peel and mash the avocados in a mixing bowl. Stir the lemon juice in immediately to prevent discoloration. Add the remaining ingredients. Slip the skins off the cooled tomato and green pepper and chop them finely. Add them to the avocado mixture, avoiding adding too much of the tomato's liquid. Mix well and chill. Serve alongside or as part of some of the dishes in this chapter, or as an appetizer dip with crisp tortilla chips.

Makes about 2 cups

SALSA VERDE (Tomatillo Sauce)

Tomatillos are members of the berry family that resemble small, green tomatoes. Their flavor is very distinct, though not hot. This recipe makes an exotic sauce for enchiladas or an offbeat dip for nachos. Look for tomatillos in cans in Mexican specialty stores.

2 tablespoons olive or safflower oil
1 medium onion, chopped
2 cloves garlic, minced
One 13-ounce can tomatillos, drained
5 or 6 sprigs cilantro or fresh
   parsley
1 to 2 tablespoons chopped mild or
   hot green chiles, to taste
½ teaspoon salt

Heat the oil in a small skillet. Add the onion and garlic and sauté until the onion is translucent. Transfer to the container of a food processor or blender along with the remaining ingredients. Process until fairly smoothly pureed.

Makes about 1 cup

SALSA RANCHERA (Raw Tomato Salsa)

This is the most basic relish of the Southwest—coarsely pureed raw tomatoes spiked with hot jalapeño peppers. Commonly used as an appetizer dip for crisp tortilla chips or nachos, it is also called for in other recipes throughout this book. This sauce is sometimes known as salsa cruda.

2 cups chopped ripe tomatoes or
   one 14-ounce can imported
   tomatoes, lightly drained
1 small onion, quartered
1 or 2 jalapeño peppers, seeded
   (see note)
5 or 6 sprigs cilantro (or substitute
   fresh parsley if necessary)
1 tablespoon lemon juice
½ teaspoon ground cumin
¼ teaspoon salt, or to taste
Freshly ground black pepper to taste

To prepare in a food processor or blender, simply place all the ingredients in the container and pulse on and off until the ingredients are coarsely pureed. To prepare by hand, mince as finely as possible the tomatoes, onion, jalapeños, and cilantro or parsley. Stir in the remaining ingredients. Store in an airtight jar. This will keep for several days, but it is best fresh.

Makes about 2 cups

NOTE: You may use fresh, canned or jarred jalapeños. Be aware that even one will render a very hot salsa, while two will make this downright incendiary. Those with more experienced palates are free to use as many jalapeños as they like.

There are all sorts of chili peppers, ranging from the kind that scorch your throat a little to the kind that burst into white flame like an atomic bomb as they go down. The hottest you can buy is the *chili jalapeño*—Chili of Jalapa. Mexicans eat it raw, and claim that it's good for digestion. God help you if you try to do the same without a long tactical training period in Mexican cookery.

—Green Peyton
San Antonio: City in the Sun, 1946

GREEN CHILE SAUCE

No matter what time of day or night, the food I ate in New Mexico was, more often than not, liberally doused with this type of sauce—nowhere else is the love of green chile more apparent. In most parts of the country other than the Southwest, it is difficult to buy the fresh or frozen Anaheim or Poblano chiles used for cooking. Thus I recommend here, and in other recipes, the canned green chiles that come from the Southwest, which are good, but come in small dosages. No matter how they come, though, green chiles are indispensable for giving southwestern recipes an authentic touch.

1 tablespoon safflower oil
1 medium onion, finely chopped
1 clove garlic, finely minced
1 tablespoon unbleached white flour
1 cup (two 4-ounce cans) green
    chiles, drained and chopped
½ cup water or liquid from the
    canned chiles
½ teaspoon salt

This chili sauce is excellent and much better and healthful than catsups.

—*Buckeye Cookery*, revised
    edition, 1885

Heat the oil in a small, heavy saucepan. Add the onion and sauté over low heat until it is translucent. Add the garlic and continue to sauté until the onion is golden. Sprinkle in the flour and cook, stirring, until the mixture begins to brown lightly. Stir in the green chiles, liquid, and salt. Simmer over very low heat, covered, for 15 minutes.

Makes about 1¼ cups

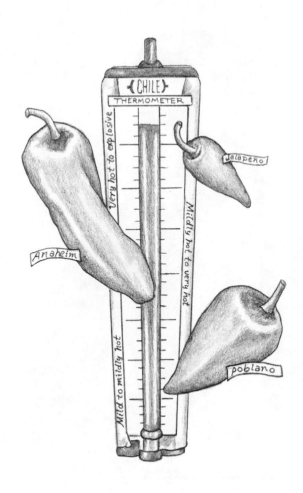

Chapter 9
DESSERTS

When you are seated next to a lady, you should only be polite during the first course; you may be gallant in the second, but you must not be tender till the dessert.

—*The New York Mirror*, 1838

The task of choosing desserts from the vast array of American goodies was absolutely mind-boggling. From all the old menus and cookbooks I pored over, there was no doubt that this has always been a country with a giant sweet tooth. The number of pies and puddings alone could fill volumes. My goal was to choose those desserts that have some intrinsically healthy quality, and as it turned out, this was easy to achieve due to the great selection of fruit desserts that have become classics. This allowed me to substantially reduce the amount of sugar used, often by as much as two-thirds, and in some cases, eliminating it almost completely.

My sweetener of choice is usually light brown sugar. Most vegetarian cookbooks use honey more often, but it has been established that it has little more nutritional value than sugar and, tablespoon for tablespoon, has more calories. Honey also tends to assert itself more and would have been inappropriate for many of these desserts. Brown sugar is nothing more than sugar colored with a little molasses, but there's more comfort in knowing that of all sweeteners, molasses is one of the few, with its good mineral content, that has any substantial food value. I was glad, then, of having had the opportunity to include some molasses-sweetened treats, such as the famous Pennsylvania Dutch Shoofly Pie and one of the enduring ancestors of American desserts, Indian Pudding.

As chronicled by Robert Beverly and William Byrd in the early 1700s, the South was a paradise of fruit and nut trees. Beverly would occasionally comment on the superiority of the native fruits over their European equivalents, saying, for example, that there were "many kinds of peaches, which have come from Europe, all of which are not nearly so good as the natural Native Indian ones, which are exceedingly good." He goes on to rhapsodize on the luscious, colorful berries and currants and provides a list of apple varieties that is unimaginable. Nut trees are similarly enumerated by Byrd.

With the availability of such produce in the New Land, combined with the already highly sophisticated dessert-making skills brought over by European women, it's no wonder that this area of cookery gained so prominent a place in the annals of American food.

So many of us are trying to cut down on sugar, but still, we occasionally want to satisfy our sweet tooth. Many of these recipes will show that it's possible to do both and that dessert can be delicious without having to be decadent as well!

BASIC PIECRUST

Making piecrust is easy, once you get the hang of it. A food processor is especially handy for making the dough, but is not essential. Double this recipe for making two-crust pies or those that call for lattice strips on top. Vegetable shortening is not as pleasant to use as butter, but it does have the advantage of having no cholesterol.

½ cup whole wheat flour
½ cup unbleached white flour
½ teaspoon salt
¼ cup (½ stick) unsalted butter, cut into bits, or ¼ cup vegetable shortening
4 to 5 tablespoons ice water

None of them will speak to you, or if they do, they are as short as pie-crust.

—William K. Northall
Before and Behind the Curtain,
1851

Combine the flours and salt.

To make by hand, place the flour mixture in a mixing bowl along with the butter or vegetable shortening. Work into the flour with a pastry blender or with the tines of a fork until the mixture resembles a coarse meal. Work the ice water in, 1 tablespoon at a time, until the dough holds together. Shape the dough into a smooth ball.

To make in a food processor, place the flour mixture in the workbowl fitted with the metal blade or with the special dough blade. Add the butter, pulsing the motor on and off several times until the butter "disappears." Add the water, 1 tablespoon at a time, through the feed tube, until the dough holds together as a mass. Remove and shape into a smooth round.

On a well-floured board, roll the dough out evenly and unformly until it is large enough to fit a 9-inch pie pan. Line the pan with the crust and trim the edges. Scallop the edges with your fingers to make it look nice. Use as directed in recipes.

Makes one 9-inch piecrust

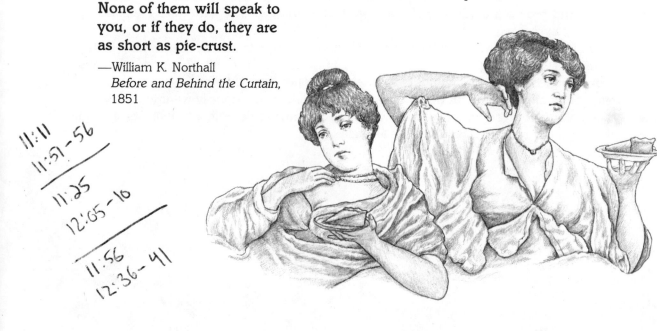

PUMPKIN OR BUTTERNUT SQUASH PIE

After the all-American apple pie, nothing so typifies the American dessert as pumpkin pie, with its familiar evocations of Thanksgiving at grandmother's house. I chose to include this standard recipe mostly to show off its lesser-known but equally venerable counterpart, the squash pie. The sweetened squash pie was also a colonial New England institution, and you'll find that the smooth, sweet butternut pulp tastes just as good as pumpkin—perhaps even better.

2 cups mashed, well-cooked
  pumpkin or butternut squash pulp
  (or use canned pumpkin if
  necessary)
2 eggs
⅔ cup firmly packed light brown
  sugar
½ cup whole milk or light cream
1 teaspoon cinnamon
1 teaspoon grated lemon rind
  (optional)
½ teaspoon ground ginger
½ teaspoon ground nutmeg
¼ teaspoon ground allspice
1 recipe Basic piecrust (page 152)

Preheat the oven to 350°F.

Place the pumpkin or squash pulp in the container of a food processor or blender with the eggs, sugar, milk or cream, and spices. Process until velvety smooth. Pour the mixture into the piecrust. Bake for 40 to 45 minutes, or until the mixture is set and the crust is golden brown. Let the pie cool to room temperature or until it is just warm.

Serves 6 to 8

Ah! On Thanksgiving day, when from East
  and from West,
From North and from South come the
  pilgrim and guest,
When the gray-haired New Englander
  sees round his board
The old broken links of affection restored,
When the care-wearied man seeks his
  mother once more,
And the worn matron smiles where the
  girl smiled before,
What moistens the lip and what brightens
  the eye?
What calls back the past, like the rich
  pumpkin pie?

—Anonymous
The New England Cookbook, 1936

BOSTON CRANBERRY PIE

This old-fashioned, lattice-stripped New England pie is very pretty to look at and offers a nice contrast between the very tart berries and the sweet raisins. Look for fresh cranberries in the produce section of your supermarket during the Thanksgiving and Christmas season.

2 tablespoons cornstarch
½ cup firmly packed light brown sugar
¼ teaspoon salt
1 cup boiling water
2 cups fresh cranberries
1 cup dark raisins
1 tablespoon butter
2 recipes Basic Piecrust (page 152), to make bottom crust plus lattice strips

Preheat the oven to 400°F.

In the top of a double boiler, combine the cornstarch, sugar, and salt. Over low heat, pour ¼ cup of the boiling water over this mixture and stir until thoroughly dissolved. Stir the remaining water in and cook, allowing it to bubble gently, until thickened. Add the cranberries, raisins, and butter and cook over low heat for 10 minutes. Allow the mixture to stand for 10 minutes, then pour it into the crust. Cover the top with lattice strips ½-inch wide, spaced about ½ inch apart. Bake for 30 to 35 minutes, or until the fruit is soft and the crust is golden. Cool to room temperature or until just warm.

Serves 6 to 8

Cranberries grow in the low lands, and barren Sunken Grounds, upon low Bushes, like the Gooseberry, and are much the same size. They are of a lively Red, when ripe, and make very good Tarts.

—Robert Beverly
The History and Present State of Virginia, 1705

BANANA CREAM PIE

Cream pies have been common since the early part of the nineteenth century, particularly in New England, but Banana Cream Pie is an early twentieth-century innovation. This pie is easy to make, but it takes some time, because there are cooling periods between the steps. Allow 1½ to 2 hours for the procedure, with baking time, plus additional time for final cooling.

1 recipe Basic Piecrust (page 152)
⅓ to ½ cup light brown sugar, to taste
2½ tablespoons unbleached white flour
1½ cups whole milk, scalded
1 egg yolk
1 teaspoon vanilla extract
Dash of nutmeg
2 large bananas, thinly sliced
2 egg whites, at room temperature
1 tablespoon granulated sugar

Preheat the oven to 350°F.

Prick a few holes in the bottom of the piecrust with a fork. Bake the crust for 15 minutes, or until golden.

Meanwhile, in the top of a double boiler, combine the brown sugar and flour. Over low heat, pour over them the scalded milk, a bit at a time. stirring very carefully so that no lumps form. Once the sugar and flour are dissolved, quickly whisk in the yolk, then stir in the vanilla and nutmeg. Cook for 15 minutes, stirring frequently, until thick and smooth. Allow both the baked crust and the filling to cool to room temperature. When nearly cooled, turn the over temperature up to 425°F.

Spoon half the cooled filling into the crust. Arrange half the banana slices in concentric circles around the pie. Repeat.

Beat the egg whites until they form stiff peaks. Sprinkle in the granulated sugar and beat briefly again. Top the pie wiith this meringue and bake for 5 minutes in the hot oven, or until touched with golden brown. Allow the pie to cool once again before serving. Serve at room temperature or chilled.

Serves 6 to 8

Variation: For a Chocolate Banana Cream Pie, simply add a 1-ounce square of unsweetened chocolate to the mixture in the double boiler after adding the egg yolk. Stir in until completely blended and continue cooking as directed.

Is it good? Sir, it is pie. It will bring to camp any idiot that sits in darkness anywhere.

—*North American Review*, 1901

SOUTHERN SWEET POTATO PIE

The product of an abundant southern crop, this classic dessert continues to be a tradition in many parts of the South.

2 cups cooked diced sweet potato
(about 1 very large potato)
2 eggs
⅔ cup firmly packed light brown
sugar
½ cup whole milk or light cream
1 tablespoon butter, melted
2 tablespoons lemon juice (optional)
1 teaspoon vanilla extract
1 teaspoon cinnamon
¼ teaspoon each: ground ginger,
ground cloves, and ground nutmeg
1 recipe Basic Piecrust (page 152)

Preheat the oven to 350°F.

Place the sweet potato dice and all the remaining ingredients (except, of course, the crust) in the container of a food processor or blender. Process until smoothly blended. Pour into the piecrust and bake for 40 to 50 minutes, or until the crust is golden and the filling is set. Serve warm.

Serves 6 to 8

There was no deficiency of custards, delicious sweet potato pies, and various wild fruits.

—Timothy Flint
George Mason, the Young Backwoodsman, 1829

PEANUT BUTTER PIE

Since peanut butter is a late-nineteenth-century innovation, it seems likely that this pie originated shortly thereafter. Most prevalent in the Middle West states, this is a rich, full-flavored pie, high in protein.

2 eggs, separated, at room
temperature
⅓ cup light brown sugar
¼ cup molasses
½ cup low-fat milk
1 teaspoon vanilla extract
½ teaspoon cinnamon
¾ cup peanut butter, at room
temperature
1 recipe Basic Piecrust (page 152)
¼ cup coarsely chopped peanuts

Preheat the oven to 350°F.

In a large mixing bowl, blend the egg yolks with the brown sugar until it dissolves. Stir in the molasses, milk, and vanilla. Add the peanut butter and beat it in vigorously with a wire whisk until smoothly blended.

Beat the egg whites until they form stiff peaks. Fold them gently into the peanut butter mixture. Pour the mixture into the piecrust and top with the chopped peanuts. Bake for 35 minutes, or until the mixture is set and the crust is golden. Serve warm or at room temperature.

Serves 6 to 8

MOCK MINCE PIE

Another pie that seems to have been prevalent in the Middle West states, Mock Mince Pie showed up in ladies' club cookbooks with as much regularity as did real mincemeat pies.

½ cup strong black coffee
1 tablespoon butter
¼ cup (scant) molasses
2 tablespoons cider vinegar
½ teaspoon vanilla extract
1 heaping cup raisins
2 medium sweet apples, peeled,
  cored, and finely chopped
¾ cup soft whole-grain bread crumbs
¼ cup finely chopped walnuts
1 teaspoon cinnamon
½ teaspoon ground allspice
¼ teaspoon ground cloves
2 recipes Basic Piecrust (page 152),
  to make bottom crust plus lattice
  strips

Pie was such a great part of the American menu that it worked its way into many common expressions. Mostly, it was used to describe anything that was the pinnacle of goodness or ease. "Easy as pie" and "as polite as pie" were ordinary phrases, as were variations of this:

He is as nice as pie this afternoon.

—G.B. McCutcheon
Green Fancy, 1917

Preheat the oven to 375°F.

In a heavy saucepan, combine the coffee, butter, molasses, and vinegar. Heat until just below the boiling point, then add the vanilla, raisins, and chopped apples and simmer over low heat for 8 to 10 minutes.

In the meantime, combine the bread crumbs, walnuts, and spices in a mixing bowl. Pour the mixture from the saucepan over the dry mixture and stir vigorously until well mixed. Pour into the piecrust and top with ½-inch-wide lattice strips, arranged ½ inch apart. Bake for 30 to 35 minutes, or until the crust is golden.

Serves 6 to 8

SHOOFLY PIE

The classic Shoofly Pie of the Pennsylvania Dutch did not become widely known to the rest of America until the late nineteenth or early twentieth century. The prevalent and rather obvious explanation for its name is that the sweet, sticky filling of the pie attracts flies, who must be shooed away. This unusual pie will please you if you enjoy the distinct, robust flavor of molasses.

Crumbs mixture:
¼ cup (½ stick) butter, softened and
  cut into bits
½ cup unbleached white flour
½ cup whole wheat flour
⅓ cup firmly packed light brown
  sugar
1 teaspoon cinnamon
¼ teaspoon each: ground ginger,
  ground cloves, and salt

½ cup molasses
½ cup boiling water
½ teaspoon baking soda
1 recipe Basic Piecrust (page 152)

Preheat the oven to 375°F.

In a mixing bowl, combine the ingredients for the crumbs mixture. Work the butter into the mixture with a fork until the dry ingredients resemble a coarse meal.

In another bowl, dissolve the molasses in the boiling water. Sprinkle in the baking soda and stir until it dissolves. Add about two-thirds of the crumbs mixture and stir together until the crumbs are moistened, but the mixture need not be smooth. Pour into the piecrust and top with the remaining crumbs. Bake for 30 to 35 minutes, or until the crust and crumbs are golden and the filling is set. Serve warm or at room temperature.

Serves 6 to 8

Amish women have debated for generations on how to keep flies off of shoo-fly pie.

PECAN SQUARES

Pecans are the number-one nut of the South and go into the making of a number of traditional desserts.

2 eggs, well beaten
½ cup firmly packed light brown
  sugar
½ cup low-fat milk
3 tablespoons butter, melted
½ cup whole wheat flour
½ cup unbleached white flour
1½ teaspoons baking powder
¼ teaspoon salt
½ teaspoon cinnamon
¼ teaspoon ground allspice
⅛ teaspoon ground cloves
1½ cups chopped pecans
½ cup currants

Preheat the oven to 350°F.

In a small mixing bowl, combine the beaten egg with the sugar and stir until the sugar is dissolved. Stir in the milk and melted butter.

In another mixing bowl, combine the flours, baking powder, salt, and spices. Slowly add the wet mixture to the dry and beat together vigorously until smoothly blended. Fold in the pecans and currants. Pour the mixture into an oiled 9-by-9-inch aluminum baking pan. Bake for 25 to 30 minutes, or until the top is golden and a knife inserted into the center tests clean. Let cool, then cut into 9 or 12 squares to serve.

CHOCOLATE BOURBON PECAN PIE

There were many pecan pies to be had as I traveled around the South, but most of the time they were simply thick beds of corn syrup with a few pecans floating on top. I prefer this variation, rich as it is—the addition of bourbon gives it a flavor of Kentucky baking.

2 eggs, beaten
½ cup light corn syrup
2 tablespoons molasses
3 tablespoons bourbon whiskey
1 teaspoon vanilla extract
⅛ teaspoon salt
1½ cups coarsely chopped pecans
1 cup semisweet chocolate chips
1 recipe Basic Piecrust (page 152)

Preheat the oven to 350°F.

In a mixing bowl, beat the eggs until light. Add the corn syrup, molasses, bourbon, and vanilla and beat together until well blended. Add the salt, pecans, and chocolate chips and stir together. Pour the mixture into the piecrust and bake for 40 to 45 minutes, or until the crust is golden and the filling is set. Serve warm.

Serves 6 to 8

SOUTHERN BLACK CAKE

This recipe, of Virginia and Maryland origins, makes a moist, dark cake with a spicy, complex flavor which was very widely traveled in the nineteenth century. General cookbooks, whether southern or not, often contained several versions from different contributors.

¼ cup (½ stick) butter, softened
⅓ cup firmly packed light brown
  sugar
2 eggs, well beaten
⅓ cup molasses
½ cup hot, strong coffee
¼ cup whole or low-fat milk
1 cup whole wheat flour
¾ cup unbleached white flour
1½ teaspoons baking powder
1 tablespoon dry, unsweetened
  cocoa
1 teaspoon cinnamon
¼ teaspoon each ground nutmeg,
  ground cloves, and ground
  allspice
¾ cup raisins

Preheat the oven to 350°F.

In a mixing bowl, cream together the butter and sugar. Add the beaten eggs and whisk together until smooth. Stir in the molasses, coffee, and milk and beat together until well blended.

In another bowl, sift together the flours, baking powder, cocoa, and spices. Add the wet ingredients gradually to the dry and stir vigorously until smoothly blended. Stir in the raisins. Pour into an oiled 9-by-9-inch aluminum baking pan. Bake for 30 to 35 minutes, or until a knife inserted into the center tests clean. Let cool and cut into 9 or 12 squares to serve.

**I hope before I'm through
To eat my cake and bake it,
too.**

—Margaret Fishback
Career Girl, 1940

HARWICH HERMITS

This New England spice cake is related to the somewhat more common "hermit cookie," whose ingredients are very similar. I enjoy the spicy flavors more in this form, and it's easier and quicker to make, too.

¼ cup (½ stick) butter, softened
¼ cup firmly packed light brown
    sugar
2 eggs, well beaten
½ cup whole or low-fat milk
⅓ cup molasses
1 cup whole wheat flour
¾ cup unbleached white flour
1½ teaspoons baking powder
½ teaspoon salt
1 teaspoon cinnamon
½ teaspoon ground cloves
¼ teaspoon ground nutmeg
⅔ cup raisins
¾ cup finely chopped walnuts

"Let all things be done decently and in order," and the first thing to put in order when you are going to bake is yourself. Secure the hair in a net or other covering, to prevent any from falling, and brush the shoulders and back to be sure none are lodged there that might blow off; make the hands and finger nails clean, roll the sleeves up above the elbows, and put on a large, clean apron.

—*The Buckeye Cookbook,* 1883

Preheat the oven to 350°F.

Cream the butter and sugar together. Add the eggs, molasses, and milk and beat together until smooth.

Sift the flours, baking powder, salt, and spices into a mixing bowl. Add the wet ingredients gradually to the dry and beat together vigorously until smoothly blended. Fold in the raisins and nuts. Pour into an oiled 9-by-9-inch aluminum baking pan. Bake for 25 to 30 minutes, or until a knife inserted into the center tests clean and the top is golden. Let cool, then cut into 9 or 12 squares to serve.

APPLE PANDOWDY

This is a very old, homey New England recipe that became well known to the rest of the country early in this century, but has since fallen mostly by the wayside. I think it's perfect to revive it in a vegetarian collection, since it is definitely a healthy dessert. The common explanation for its somewhat silly name (which should be taken with a grain of salt!) is that it's due to its being a plain, simple, and therefore "dowdy" dish.

5 heaping cups thinly sliced peeled
    tart apples
¼ cup maple syrup
¼ teaspoon each cinnamon, ground
    cloves, and ground nutmeg

Batter:
⅔ cup whole wheat flour
⅓ cup unbleached white flour
1¼ teaspoon baking powder
½ teaspoon cinnamon
¼ teaspoon salt
1 egg, beaten
¼ cup firmly packed light brown
    sugar
3 tablespoons butter, melted
½ cup whole or low-fat milk
¼ cup finely chopped walnuts

Vanilla ice cream (optional)

Preheat the oven to 350°F.

Combine the apple slices, syrup, and spices in a bowl and stir together until the apples are coated. Arrange in a buttered 1½-quart baking casserole and bake, covered, for 20 minutes.

Sift together into a mixing bowl the flours, baking powder, cinnamon, and salt. In another bowl, beat the egg together with the sugar, melted butter, and milk until well blended. Stir the wet mixture into the dry and beat together vigorously until smooth.

Sprinkle the nuts over the apples, then pour the batter over them and pat it in. Bake, uncovered for 30 to 35 minutes, or until nicely browned. This is best served fresh and warm and is delicious with vanilla ice cream.

Serves 6 to 8

In the eighteenth and nineteenth centuries, America was an apple-loving nation. There must have been dozens and dozens, if not hundreds, of distinct varieties. Along with these also developed quite a number of "apple sayings." Here are just a few:

Victorian girls with healthy coloring were referred to as "apple-cheeked."

At the turn of the twentieth century, "go climb a sour apple tree" was a way of telling someone to go to the devil!

In the roaring twenties, yes-men came to be known as "apple polishers."

APPLE BROWN BETTY

Another healthy apple dessert, this recipe has been known since colonial times and is also known as Apple Betty or Apple Crisp. The beauty of this recipe is that it's so naturally sweet. In old recipes, the crumbs are usually just plain bread crumbs, but I've updated the mixture by adding high-protein wheat germ and nuts.

Crumbs mixture:

½ cup soft whole-grain bread crumbs
½ cup wheat germ
½ cup finely chopped pecans or walnuts
1 tablespoon light brown sugar
¼ teaspoon cinnamon
2 tablespoons butter, melted

⅓ cup apple juice
1 teaspoon cinnamon
¼ teaspoon each: ground cloves and ground allspice or ground nutmeg
4 large sweet apples (such as Cortlandt), peeled, cored, and thinly sliced
½ cup raisins
Vanilla ice cream (optional)

Preheat the oven to 350°F.

Combine the ingredients for the crumbs mixture in a small bowl and stir together until evenly coated with the melted butter.

In another mixing bowl, combine the apple juice with the spices, then add the apple slices and raisins and stir until the apples are evenly coated.

Sprinkle the bottom of an oiled 9-by-9-inch baking pan with a light layer of the crumbs mixture. Pour in half the apple mixture, followed by half the crumbs. Repeat. Bake, covered, for 35 to 40 minutes, or until the apples are pierced easily with a fork. Uncover and bake for an additional 10 minutes. Like Apple Pandowdy, this is best served warm with vanilla ice cream.

Serves 6

Yes, sir...great idea, sir....that's brilliant, sir...true, sir...yes, sir

A classic "apple-polisher" with boss

STRAWBERRY FLUMMERY

Flummery is a nonsense word of Welsh and English origins that came to define a food made by coagulation. Here in the United States the name and the practice were continued with thickened milk usually served with sweetened fruit. This cornstarch-thickened version has come to be associated with the Shakers and has been included in several collections as "Sister Abigail's Strawberry Flummery." I have modified the original recipe by folding the berries into the thickened milk rather than setting them on top, thus reducing significantly the amount of sugar needed. This is a wonderful, elegant dessert that is, I think, even nicer than strawberries with heavy cream.

2 cups whole milk
3 to 4 tablespoons granulated sugar, to taste
¼ cup cornstarch
Pinch of salt
½ teaspoon vanilla extract
1 pint sweet, ripe strawberries, hulled and finely chopped
1 tablespoon lemon juice (optional)

All the woods, fields and gardens are full of strawberries, which grow excellently well in this beautiful and lovely land.

—William Byrd
Natural History of Virginia, 1737

Scald 1½ cups of the milk in a double boiler by bringing it to just under the boiling point (alternatively, use a heavy saucepan with 2 burner rings underneath).

In the meantime, combine the sugar, cornstarch, and salt in a small bowl and moisten them slowly with the remaining ½ cup of milk. Stir until thoroughly dissolved, then pour slowly into the scalded milk. Cook over very low heat for 10 to 15 minutes, or until smooth and thick. Remove from the heat.

Let the mixture cool for 10 minutes, then stir in the strawberries and the optional lemon juice, if you'd like a slight tang. Turn the mixture out into a 1-quart serving bowl or 6 individual dessert cups. Refrigerate until well chilled.

Serves 6

STRAWBERRY SHORTCAKE

There were many different types of shortcake in nineteenth-century baking, some like stacked pancakes to be eaten with sauce and some that were almost like plain biscuits. This recipe, adapted from one of my favorite cooks of that century, Miss Parloa, is the old-fashioned predecessor of today's strawberry shortcake—simply crushed, sweetened fruit between two rounds of warm dough.

¾ cup whole wheat flour
¾ cup unbleached white flour
1½ teaspoons baking powder
½ teaspoon salt
⅓ cup plus 3 tablespoons firmly
  packed light brown sugar
2 tablespoons butter, melted
¾ cup low-fat milk
1 pint sweet, ripe strawberries,
  hulled and crushed
Heavy cream (optional)

Preheat the oven to 400°F.

In a mixing bowl, sift together the flours, baking powder, and salt. In another bowl, combine ⅓ cup of the sugar with the melted butter until it dissolves. Stir in the milk, then combine the wet with the dry ingredients and work them together to form a soft dough. Turn the dough out onto a well-floured board and knead for a minute or so. Divide the dough into 2 equal parts, form into smooth balls, and roll out to fit the bottom of a pie pan. Place the rounds of dough in 2 lightly oiled pie pans. Bake for 12 to 15 minutes, or until the dough is golden.

In the meantime, combine the crushed strawberries with the remaining 3 tablespoons sugar in a small bowl. Cover until ready to use.

Allow the baked dough to cool until it is just warm to the touch. Place one round on a serving plate, spread it with the berries, and top with the other round of dough. Cut into wedges to serve; this is best served fresh and warm. Top each serving with a bit of cold, stiffly beaten heavy cream if you'd like.

Serve 6

Strawberries they have, as delicious as any in the world, and growing almost everywhere in the Woods and Fields. They are eaten by almost all Creatures; and yet they are so plentiful that very few Persons take care to transplant them, but can find enough to fill their Baskets, when they have a mind, in the deserted old fields.

—Robert Beverly
The History and Present State of Virginia, 1705

BAKED INDIAN PUDDING

This has to be the grandmother of all American desserts, having been among the earliest of cornmeal recipes that the Indians taught the colonists. Amazingly, this can still be had in many fine New England restaurants. I was unsure about including this recipe, in fact, until I tried it while eating out and was convinced. It's a real culinary wonder, considering that this is basically milk, cornmeal, and molasses. Keep in mind that you need 2½ hours of baking time, but you adventurous cooks must try it just for the experience! Vanilla ice cream, melting all over this dark, mysterious pudding, is a must.

4 cups (1 quart) whole or low-fat milk
1½ tablespoons butter, cut into bits
⅛ teaspoon salt
⅓ cup cornmeal
⅓ cup molasses
1 large egg, well beaten
¼ cup firmly packed light brown sugar
½ teaspoon ground ginger
½ teaspoon cinnamon
¼ cup raisins (optional)
Vanilla ice cream

Preheat the oven to 300°F.

In a double boiler, scald 3 cups of the milk by bringing it to just under the boiling point. Stir in the butter to melt and add the salt. Very slowly and patiently, sprinkle in the cornmeal, stirring continuously. You must be extra-careful to avoid lumping. Stir in the molasses and cook over very low heat for 20 minutes, or until thick and smooth. Remove from the heat.

Combine the beaten egg with the sugar until it dissolves. Add the ginger, cinnamon, and optional raisins, and add this to the cornmeal mixture. Stir until thoroughly blended. Pour into an oiled 1½-quart baking casserole.

Bake for 30 minutes, then pour the remaining 1 cup milk over the top but do not stir it in. Bake for another 2 hours. Serve warm in bowls, topped by a scoop of vanilla ice cream.

Serves 6

Then again there was the Indian baked pudding made of ambrosia, milk, and eggs, with a trifle of Muscovado sugar or Portorique molasses. I can remember when I could eat near upon a six-quart pan of this delicious viand and then cry for more.

—Thomas Robinson Hazard
The Jonny-Cake Papers of "Shepherd Tom,"
1915

BREAD PUDDING WITH WHISKEY SAUCE

This sumptuous dessert is a New Orleans classic, still served in many restaurants. A good amount of a heavy, buttery sauce is usually poured over each serving; in my version, a small amount of sauce is baked right into the pudding, making it considerably lighter.

1 good-sized loaf of French or
    Italian bread, 1 or 2 days old
2 cups whole or low-fat milk
2 eggs, beaten
2 teaspoons vanilla extract
⅓ cup light brown sugar
¾ cup raisins

Sauce:
3 tablespoons butter
2 tablespoons light brown sugar
¼ cup bourbon whiskey

Preheat the oven to 350°F.

Cut the bread into 1-inch cubes. Place them in a mixing bowl and pour the milk over them. With your hands, squeeze the milk through the bread cubes until they are soaked and all or most of the milk is absorbed. In a small bowl, beat together the eggs with the vanilla, then stir in the sugar until it is absorbed. Add this to the bread mixture and stir together quickly. Fold in the raisins.

Butter a 1½-quart baking casserole, pour the bread mixture in and pat it in smoothly. Bake for 30 minutes. Melt the butter in a small saucepan. Add the sugar, stirring until it dissolves, then remove from the heat and stir in the whiskey. Spoon the sauce evenly over the bread pudding, then bake for another 10 minutes, or until the top is golden brown and the pudding is nicely puffed. Serve warm.

Serves 6

BLACKBERRY OR BLUEBERRY COBBLER

This classic dessert, traditional to several regions, is delicious on its own or with vanilla ice cream.

1 pint fresh blackberries or
    blueberries
⅓ to ½ cup light brown sugar, to
    taste
½ cup whole wheat flour
½ cup unbleached white flour
1½ teaspoons baking powder
¼ teaspoon salt
1 egg, well beaten
¾ cup low-fat milk
2 tablespoons butter, melted

Preheat the oven to 400°F.

Wash the berries and make sure that they are thoroughly picked over. In a mixing bowl, toss them with a little less than half the sugar. Place the berries in a buttered 9-by-9-inch baking pan.

In the same mixing bowl, stir together the flours, baking powder, and salt. In a small bowl, add the remaining sugar to the beaten egg. Stir this mixture into the flour mixture and slowly add the milk, then the melted butter. Stir vigorously until smoothly blended. Pour the batter evenly over the berries. Bake for 30 to 35 minutes, or until the berries are soft and the batter is golden. Serve warm.

Serves 6.

STEWED SPICED PEARS IN RED WINE

Although stewing fruits in wine has a decidedly European background, it has become an American classic due to its early adoption by southern cooks. An absolutely delicious and elegant way to present pears, this is especially nice in the winter when so few other fruits are available.

5 large Bosc pears
⅓ cup dry red wine
⅓ cup apple juice
¼ lemon, cut into small bits, including the rind
6 whole cloves
1 small cinnamon stick, broken in half
¼ teaspoon ground allspice
1 tablespoon cornstarch, dissolved in 3 tablespoons water

Pears and peaches ain't often found on the same tree, I tell you.

—Thomas C. Haliburton
The Attache, or Sam Slick in England, 1843

Stem the pears and cut them into quarters lengthwise. Core them and divide the quarters in half again lengthwise. In a deep, heavy saucepan, combine all the ingredients except the cornstarch and pears. Over low heat, bring the mixture to just under the boiling point. Slowly pour in the dissolved cornstarch, then stir in the pear slices. Cover and simmer over very low heat until the pears are tender, stirring occasionally. When the pears are done, they should be easily pierced with a fork, but still firm enough to retain their shape. This will take anywhere from 25 to 45 minutes, depending on the size and ripeness of the pears. If there seems to be too much liquid in the saucepan once the pears are done, cook, uncovered, for 5 to 10 minutes until it is reduced. This is best served just warm.

Serves 4 to 6.

UNBAKED PEACH CRISP

The first thing I remember seeing when driving into South Carolina was a giant peach on a pedestal that seemed to reach the sky. Peaches are one of the hallmark fruits of the South, and many of its classic recipes developed there. I decided to alter this standard a bit; I love peaches but dislike how they taste baked—they seem to lose all their flavor, and their juiciness turns to mush. I hope you'll agree that this modification does justice to the peach. The result is a healthy dessert that's very low in sugar.

2 tablespoons butter
5 or 6 good-sized, juicy sweet
    peaches, thinly sliced
1 to 2 tablespoons light brown
    sugar, to taste
1 teaspoon cinnamon
½ cup rolled oats
⅓ cup wheat germ
⅓ cup raisins
⅛ teaspoon ground cloves
Vanilla ice cream (optional)

Heat half the butter in a large skillet. Add the sliced peaches and sauté over low heat for 5 minutes. Stir in the sugar until it dissolves, then sprinkle in half the cinnamon. Turn the peaches into a 9-by-9-inch pan and pat them in.

Heat a dry skillet and toast the oats in it over moderate heat, stirring frequently, until they are golden brown. Add the wheat germ and the remaining butter and stir until the butter is evenly melted throughout. Stir in the raisins, the remaining cinnamon, and the cloves. Sprinkle this mixture evenly over the peaches and pat it in. Allow to cool to room temperature. Serve on its own or over vanilla ice cream.

Serves 6.

MENUS

The following menus, built around seasons, regional themes or special occasions, offer an idea as to how the individual recipes might be incorporated into meals. In all cases, dessert is entirely optional—I prefer having fruit after everyday meals and saving desserts for special occasions, such as when I have guests for supper.

SUPPERS WITH REGIONAL THEMES

Southern Suppers for Spring

BAKED CHEESE GRITS (page 94)
POTATOES WITH COLLARD GREENS (page 124)
STRING BEANS WITH TOMATOES AND BASIL (page 132)
Honeydew melon

HOPPING-JOHN (page 106)
BUTTERMILK-CORN BREAD (page xx) or HOMINY MUFFINS (page 28)
NORTH CAROLINA RELISH SLAW (page 65)
STRING BEANS WITH LEMON AND GARLIC (page 132)
BLACKBERRY COBBLER (page 167)

A Southern Supper for Fall or Winter

SOUTHERN LIMA BEANS (page 104)
RICE-AND-CORNMEAL SPOONBREAD (page 41)
Seasonal mixed salad
Baked butternut squash
APPLE BROWN BETTY (page 163)

A New England Supper for Summer

CORN PUDDING (page 90)
HARVARD BEETS (page 113)
POTATO SALAD WITH OLD-FASHIONED BOILED DRESSING (page 69)
Sliced sweet red bell pepper
BLUEBERRY COBBLER (page 167)

A New England Supper for Winter

FARMER'S CABBAGE (page 119)
BAKED SWEET POTATOES AND APPLES (page 123)
Simple salad of mixed greens with grated sharp Cheddar cheese
BOSTON CRANBERRY PIE (page 154)

A Pennsylvania Dutch Supper for Fall or Winter

DUTCH SUCCOTASH (page 92)
RED WINE CABBAGE (page 118)
Sliced cucumbers with fresh dill in yogurt
SHOOFLY PIE (page 158)

A Creole Supper for Summer, Fall, or Winter

CREOLE EGGPLANT SOUP (page 48)
RICE MUFFINS (page 20)
Seasonal mixed salad
STUFFED MIRLITON (page 128, for summer)
or
PECAN-STUFFED SQUASH (page 126, for fall or winter)
SOUTHERN BLACK CAKE (page 160)
or
Fruit in season

A Late Spring or Early Summer Creole Supper for Company

BUTTERMILK BISCUITS (page 18)
EGGPLANT SOUFFLÉ (page 114)
CREOLE OKRA AND TOMATOES (page 116)
Fresh green peas, steamed and minted
Simple green salad
BREAD PUDDING WITH WHISKEY SAUCE (page 167)

A Simple Creole Supper for Spring or Fall

This is a good meal to make on a rainy Sunday, as both the beans and the beets take a long time to cook.

RED BEANS AND RICE (page 99)
BEETS PIQUANTE (page 112)
Seasonal mixed salad
PECAN SQUARES (page 159)
or
Fruit in season

SOUTHWESTERN SUPPERS

Since these meals tend to be filling, I suggest a light dessert of a cooling sherbet or a colorful fruit salad dressed in yogurt with a touch of honey if you are serving guests.

BAKED RICE WITH CHEESE AND GREEN CHILES (page 108)
FRIJOLES BORRACHOS (page 100)
Sautéed chayote (vegetable pear) or zucchini
Diced tomatoes drizzled with olive oil

GREEN CHILE ENCHILADAS (page 137)
or
GUACAMOLE ENCHILADAS (page 138)
POSOLE (Spanish Hominy, page 95)
or
MEXICAN RICE (page 109)
Seasonal mixed salad

CHILAQUILES (Tortilla Casserole, page 140)
SPANISH-STYLE GARBANZOS (page 101)
CALAVACITAS (Summer Squash with Corn, page 130)
Shredded lettuce and black olives

SOUP AND SALAD SUPPERS

I have a penchant for meals built around soup, salad, and a good bread. Here are a few suggestions. Dessert is, of course, optional but a fruity dessert is a good bet.

For Any Season

ZUCCHINI CHOWDER (page 56)
SOUTHWESTERN RICE SALAD (page 74)
ZUNI QUICK BREAD (page 35)

BLACK BEAN SOUP (page 47)
SHAKER CHEDDAR BREAD (page 38)
Seasonal mixed salad

VIRGINIA PEANUT SOUP (page 55)
CORN-RELISH SALAD (page 68)
CAROLINA RICE-AND-WHEAT BREAD (page 32)

For Summer

CHILLED AVOCADO SOUP (page 58)
TEXAS CAVIAR (Marinated Black-eyed Peas, page 71)
BUTTERMILK-CORN BREAD (page 28)

For Early Fall

SWEET POTATO SOUP (page 50)
JERUSALEM ARTICHOKE SALAD (page 67)
Sliced tomatoes and green bell peppers
HOMINY MUFFINS (page 20)

SQUASH-AND CORN-CHOWDER (page 59)
CAULIFLOWER AND AVOCADO SALAD (page 75)
POTATO BISCUITS (page 19)

For Winter

RED BEAN SOUP (page 46)
CABBAGE-AND-PEPPER SLAW (page 64)
RICE MUFFINS (page 20)

SPECIAL BRUNCHES

Breakfast in New Orleans

EGGS CREOLE (page 84)
BUTTERMILK BISCUITS (page 18)
Cooked grits, lightly buttered
PECAN SQUARES (page 159) and fresh fruit

An Elegant Brunch for Company

ARKANSAS BOILED-EGG PIE (page 83)
PARSLEY-POTATO CROQUETTES (page 123)
APPLE MUFFINS (page 21)
Mixed fruit salad with yogurt and honey

Three Brunches with a Southwestern Theme

CALIFORNIA OMELET (page 82)
GREEN CHILE CORN BREAD (page 29)
Salad of greens, tomatoes, and avocado
BLACKBERRY COBBLER (page 167), in season

MEXICAN OMELET (page 79)
FLOUR TORTILLAS (page 143), served warm
FRIJOLES REFRITOS (Refried Beans, page 97)
Cantaloupe and honeydew, in season

HUEVOS RANCHEROS (Ranch-Style Eggs, page 78)
POTATOES WITH GREEN CHILE (page 125)
Crisp raw fresh vegetables
UNBAKED PEACH CRISP (page 169), in season

MENUS FOR SPECIAL OCCASIONS

A Vegetarian Thanksgiving

ANADAMA BREAD (page 30)
VIRGINIA PEANUT SOUP (page 55)
CABBAGE-AND-PEPPER SLAW (page 64)
POTATO-BREAD STUFFING (page 121)
CREOLE EGGPLANT SOUFFLÉ (page 114)
Steamed broccoli, zucchini, and carrots
BUTTERNUT SQUASH OR PUMPKIN PIE (page 153)
STEWED SPICED PEARS IN RED WINE (page 168)
Vanilla ice cream

A Summer Picnic of Various Salads

POTATO SALAD WITH OLD-FASHIONED BOILED DRESSING (page 69)
CORN RELISH SALAD (page 68)
SUMMER SQUASH AND STRING BEAN SALAD (page 72)
ZUNI QUICK BREAD (page 35)
Cherry tomatoes
HARWICH HERMITS (page 161)
Fresh berries

A Summer Supper for a Crowd to Eat Outdoors

If you don't have a grill, you might simply wrap the vegetables in foil and bake them in the oven at the same time as the beans. Double any recipes as needed, depending on the number of eaters.

BAKED BARBECUE BEANS (page 105)

Grilled vegetables, including corn on the cob, green and red bell peppers, onions, broccoli, cauliflower, and potatoes

GREEN CHILE CORN BREAD (page 29)

CREAMY COLE SLAW (page 66)

TACO SALAD (page 73)

BLACKBERRY OR BLUEBERRY COBBLER (page 167)

Watermelon

SELECTED SOURCES

The following is a list of the books that were the most helpful among the scores I went through. There was considerable overlapping in recipes books, and many of my adaptations are composites of several versions of classic recipes. However, in certain cases, a recipe was inspired more specifically from one source, and in such cases I mention the recipe by name when a certain book was particularly valuable. Books that provided additional lore and literature to accompany the recipes, beyond those cited on the pages themselves, are also listed here.

Barringer, Maria M. *Dixie Cookery*. New York: R. Worthington, 1882 (Rice Muffins, Lace-Edged Cornmeal Batter Cakes).

Bergen, Fanny D., ed. *Animal and Plant Lore*. Boston: Houghton Mifflin/American Folklore Society, 1899.

Beverly, Robert. *The History and Present State of Virginia*. Reprint of 1705 edition. Chapel Hill, N.C.: University of North Carolina Press, 1947.

Botkin, Benjamin A. *A Treasury of New England Folklore*. New York: Crown Publishers, Inc., 1964.

Bowles, Ella S., and Towle, Dorothy. *Secrets of New England Cooking*. New York: M. Barrows & Co., 1947.

Brown, Nellie I. *Recipes from Old Hundred: Two Hundred Years of New England Cooking*. New York: M. Barrows & Co., 1939 (Old-Fashioned Oat Bread).

Buckeye Cookbook, The. Originally titled *Practical Housekeeping: A Careful Compilation of Tried and Approved Recipes*. Minneapolis: Buckeye Publishing Co., 1883 (Southern Black Cake).

Burdette, Kay. *Cookery of the Old South*. Self-published, no date (Sweet Potato Biscuits, Squash Soufflé).

Byrd, William. *Natural History of Virginia*. Translation of 1737 edition by Richard C. Beatty and William J. Malloy. Richmond, Va.: Dietz Press, 1940.

Christian Women's Exchange. *The Creole Cookery Book*. New Orleans: T. H. Thompson, 1885 (Creole Stuffed Eggplant).

Colquitt, Harriet R. *The Savannah Cookbook*. Olmstead, N.Y., 1933.

Dictionary of Americanisms. Chicago: The University of Chicago Press, 1966.

Eustic, Celestine. *Cooking in Old Creole Days*. New York: R. K. Russell, 1903 (Okra-Rice Soup).

Flexner, Marion W. *Dixie Dishes*. Boston: Hale, Cushman and Flint, 1941 (Stewed Spiced Pears in Red Wine).

Flexner, Stuart Berg. *I Hear America Talking*. New York: Simon and Schuster, 1976.

Frederick, J. George. *The Pennsylvania Dutch and Their Cookery*. Philadelphia: The Business Bourse, 1935 (Dutch Corn-and-Cabbage Soup, Dutch Succotash, Pennsylvania Dutch Corn Noodles, Red Wine Cabbage, Parsnip Croquettes, and Potato-Bread Stuffing).

Frost, Annie, ed. *The Godey's Lady's Book Receipts*. Philadelphia: Evans, Stoddart & Co., 1870.

Gilbert, Fabiola Cabeza de Baca. *The Good Life: New Mexican Food*. Santa Fe, N. M.: San Vincente Foundation, 1949.

Good, Frank, ed. *Rare Recipes and Budget Savers*. Wichita, Kans.: Wichita Eagle and Beacon, 1961.

Hearn, Lafcadio. *"Gombo Zhebes": Little Dictionary of Creole Proverbs Selected from Six Creole Dialects*. New York: W. H. Coleman, 1885.

Hibben, Sheila. *The National Cookbook: A Kitchen Americana*. New York: Harper & Bros., 1932.

Hiller, Elizabeth O. *The Corn Cookbook*. Chicago: P. F. Volland Co., 1918 (Molasses Corn Bread, Scalloped Corn, Corn Relish Salad).

Kaufman, William I., and Cooper, Sister Mary Ursula. *The Art of Creole Cookery.* New York: Doubleday & Co., 1962.

Kitchen Guild of the Tullie Smith House Restoration. *Tullie's Receipts.* Atlanta, Ga.: Atlanta Historical Society, 1976.

Ladies of the Second Presbyterian Church. *Recipes of Georgia Housekeepers.* New York: Trow's Printing and Bookbinding Co., 1883 (Corn Pudding).

Land, Mary. *Louisiana Cookery.* New York: Bonanaza Books (Crown Publishers, Inc.), 1954.

Leslie, Eliza. *Directions for Cookery in Its Various Branches.* 49th edition. Philadelphia: Henry C. Baird, 1853 (Sally Lunn Bread).

Mariani, John F. *The Dictionary of American Food and Drink.* New York: Ticknor & Fields, 1983.

Maylie, Eugenie Lavedan. *Maylie's Table d'Hote Recipes.* New Orleans: Self-published, 195-? (Cowpeas with Corn and Rice, Southern Lima Beans).

Morrow, Kay. *The New England Cookbook of Fine Old Recipes.* Reading, Pa.: Culinary Arts Press, 1936 (Creamy Cole Slaw, Maine Rye Pancakes, Boston Cranberry Pie).

New Mexico College of Agriculture. *Historic Cookery.* Santa Fe, N. M.: Agricultural Extension Service, May 1939 (Pinto Bean Salad, Potatoes with Green Chile, Quelites).

Parloa, Maria. *Miss Parloa's Kitchen Companion.* Boston: Estes and Lauriat, 1887 (Hominy Muffins, Scalloped Cauliflower, Apple Brown Betty, Strawberry Shortcake, Butternut Squash or Pumpkin Pie).

Penner, Lucille Recht. *The Colonial Cookbook.* New York: Hastings House, 1976.

Piercy, Caroline. *The Shaker Cook-Book.* New York: Crown Publishers, Inc., 1953.

Porter, Mrs. M. E. *Mrs. Porter's New Southern Cookery Book.* Philadelphia: John E. Porter & Co., 1871.

Randolph, Mary. *The Virginia Housewife.* Edited by Karen Hess. Facsimile of 1824 edition. Columbia, S.C.: University of South Carolina Press, 1984 (Tomato-Barley Soup).

Rice Industry. *Rice: Two Hundred Delightful Ways to Serve It.* New Orleans: Southern Rice Industry, 1937 (Rice-and-Cornmeal Batter Cakes, Rice-and-Cornmeal Spoonbread).

Rutledge, Sarah (attributed to). *The Carolina Housewife.* Charleston, S.C.: W. R. Babcock, 1951 (Sweet Potato Pone, Carolina Rice-and-Wheat Bread, Corn Oysters, Spoonbread, Philpy).

Scott, Natalie V. *Two Hundred Years of New Orleans Cooking.* New York: Jonathan Cape, 1931 (Rice Croquettes, Beets Piquante, Creole Okra and Tomatoes).

Simmons, Amelia. *American Cookery.* Edited by Gail Weesner. Facsimile of 1796 edition. Boston: Rowan Tree Press, 1982.

Stern, Jane and Michael. *Goodfood.* New York: Alfred A. Knopf, 1983.

Taylor, Archer, and Whiting, Bartlett J. *A Dictionary of American Proverbs and Proverbial Expressions, 1820–1880.* Cambridge, Mass.: Harvard University Press, 1967.

Taylor, Joe Gray. *Eating, Drinking and Visiting in the Old South.* Baton Rouge, La.: Louisiana State University Press, 1982.

Trinity Mission. *Out of Vermont Kitchens.* Burlington, Vt.: Trinity Mission, 1939 (Apple Muffins).

Tyree, Marion Cabell. *Housekeeping in Old Virginia.* Louisville, Ky.: John P. Morton & Co., 1870.

Works Progress Administration. *Gumbo Ya-Ya: A Collection of Louisiana Folk-Tales.* New York: Bonanza Books, Crown Publishers, Inc., 1945.

Works Progress Administration. *Louisiana: A Guide to the State.* Boston: Houghton Mifflin Co., 1938.

ACKNOWLEDGMENTS

Grateful acknowledgment is given to the following publishers for permission to reprint or adapt copyrighted materials from original sources. Best efforts were made to obtain permissions; please refer any corrections to Ballantine Books, Inc., for future editions.

American Heritage Publishing Co., New York:
From *The American Heritage Cookbook*, by the editors of *American Heritage*, © 1980: Black Bean Soup and Shoofly Pie, adapted by permission.

Arthur H. Clark Co., Glendale, Calif.:
From *Early California Hospitality* by Ana Begue de Packman, © 1938: California Omelet, Frijoles Refritos, Colache, Ejotes and Ensalada de Verduras, adapted by permission.

Doubleday & Co., Inc., Garden City, N.Y.:
From *The Art of American Indian Cooking* by Jean Anderson and Yeffe Kimball, © 1965: Jerusalem Artichoke Salad, adapted by permission.

From *Recipes from America's Restored Villages* by Jean Anderson, © 1975: Brethren Cheddar Bread and Arkansas Boiled-Egg Pie, adapted by permission.

Harper & Row, New York:
From *Cuisines of the American Southwest* by Anne Lindsay Greer, © 1983: Cold Rice Salad and Cauliflower Salad, adapted by permission.

Little, Brown & Co., Boston:
From *How Many Miles to Galena?* by Richard Bissell, © 1968: A passage entitled "There's a Salad on the Floor," reprinted by permission.

Macmillan & Co., Inc., New York:
From *The Best of Shaker Cookery* by Amy Bess Miller and Persis W. Fuller, © 1970: Herb Bread and Hancock Dill Bread, adapted by permission.

Museum of New Mexico Press, Santa Fe, N. M.:
From *The Pueblo Indian Cookbook* by Phyllis Hughes, © 1972, 1977: Zuni Bread and Rio Corn Pie, adapted by permission.

New Directions Publishing Corp., New York:
From *A Member of the Wedding* by Carson McCullers, © 1946: A passage on "Hopping-John," reprinted by permission.

Random House, Inc., New York:
From *The New England Cookbook* by Eleanor Early, © 1954: Harwich Hermits and "Farmer's Cabbage," adapted by permission.

The Times-Picayune Publishing Co., Inc.
From *The Original Picayune Creole Cookbook, © 1901* by The Times Picayune Publishing Co., 1947 edition; Potage Maigre d'Hiver, Potage Maigre d'Été, Red Bean Soup, and Potage Crecy, adapted by permission.

Vintage Books, Inc., New York:
From *American Food: The Gastronomic Story* by Evan Jones, © 1981: Objjway Butternut Squash and Corn Chowder, adapted by permission.

INDEX

ABOUT THE AUTHOR

Nava Atlas is an illustrator and graphic designer with a long-standing interest in creative natural foods cookery. The author of several vegetarian cookbooks, including *Vegetariana* and *Vegetarian Celebrations*, she lives in upstate New York with her husband and two young sons.